Gentle, Effective Parenting To Raise Thriving Children

How to be the Connected Parent with Effective Discipline and Emotional Regulation Skills; Master Your Emotions and Understand your Child.

Rosie Sutton

Little Nest Books

While we try to teach our children all about life, our children teach us what life is all about.

— *Angela Schwindt*

Special Bonus!

Want this bonus book for free?

Get FREE, unlimited access to it and all of my new books by joining the Little Nest Books Fan Base!

*Scan with your **camera** to join!*

Contents

Gentle, Effective Parenting To Raise Thriving Children

Rosie **Sutton**

ISBN 979-8-9886665-0-9 (paperback)

ISBN 979-8-9886665-2-3 (hardcover)

ISBN 979-8-9886665-3-0 (ebook)

Published by Little Nest Books

www.littlenestbooks.com

Introduction

"We liberate children, not by making them work for our love, but by letting them rest in it."

Dr. Gordon Neufeld.

Imagine this: It's a relaxing Sunday morning. You've had an exhausting week managing your home and work; today, you just want to relax, maybe get a nice cup of hot coffee and read that book you've been putting off for so many days. You sigh luxuriously and walk into the library room beside the bedroom. The second you step inside, you see your precious books strewn around the floor. Pages are opened, spines are upturned, it's a bookworm's nightmare, and you know who is responsible. You close your eyes and take two deep breaths. You're already quite familiar with your child's love of leaving the books she reads lying all around the home.

You've told her not to do it a million times, but it's always fallen just shy of enough. So, what do you do next? The peace you felt is about a second away from getting shattered. You're pretty mad— I mean, parenthood is beautiful, but books never seem to prepare you for this kind of implicit messiness. Against the jarring mic going off in your mind, "Shout! Just scream at them!" you calm down. Once you are cool enough, you get an idea that would work brilliantly well. You take some time and place all the books in a curved row leading up to the bookshelf. Then, you call your child.

You tell her that before she gets on with her day, you're going to play a game of Hansel and Gretel, where she's Gretel. To win the game, she has to lift all the books. You tell her they're the metaphorical pieces of bread the siblings from the fairytale dropped in the forest. Of course, it's a game, so her interest is piqued. However, she realizes it's pretty time-consuming soon enough. The pursuit begins from the living room. She picks up book after book, bringing them back to the shelf, arranging them, and going back to pick the next one until each book is back where it was supposed to be.

Ultimately, she looks at you, her face all puffy and red, tired, but with a lesson learned. You smile. "So, the next time you leave books lying around, we'll play this game again, okay?" Not that this is foolproof, but it gets the job done. The learning your children get from you should, as much as possible, impact the people they grow up to become. And while parenthood will always be among the sweetest and most beautiful things you ever experience, it will also be excruciatingly frustrating and maddeningly tiring. Perhaps this is because nothing worth having comes easy.

So, if anything falls short of what you want to see in an adult human being, ask yourself— "Would I want my child to grow up into this kind of a person?" What if parenting didn't involve a constant battle where you're constantly stressed, anxious, and worried that you'd have to shout or use negative reinforcements to make your child understand something? You don't want to— in fact, you abhor the principles and anger governing some of the responses involving you and your children— but you don't know what else will work.

In 2019, a study found that there is a form of parenting that can *actually reduce anxiety.* You read that right! This form is key to promoting regulated responses in ways that do not contribute to or increase the stresses of both the parents and their toddlers (Grady, 2019). Another study found the same parenting method can improve the bond you share with your child and increase the flow of love, making children appreciate the time and support of their parents as invaluable (Winston & Chicot, 2016).

Children, especially very young ones, always mirror what they see. The habits they inculcate as toddlers and tweens often get rooted into their systems, propelling behavioral traits that become core to their nature later on. The form of parenting I've just highlighted is enmeshed in empathy and respect. It is *gentle parenting,* a way for your children to learn and model the positive habits you instill in them. You are raising them wholesomely and opening their minds to the likelihood of grasping the power of being empathic and respectful human beings.

Suppose you've found your way to this book. In that case, I'm going to go out on a limb and say you genuinely wish to raise well-behaved children and instill discipline in a balanced way— your child shouldn't see you as a pushover, but neither should they be terrified by you. You want a resource to show you the way when stepping away from toxic generational cycles. Hence, you act and respond in healthy ways. You don't consciously crave a household torn apart by petty fights and arguments. But it's proving tricky because your children are at that age when their very rubric is defined by unruliness.

They're tricky to manage, and your tendency to question all that you do isn't helping. You have done the research, and by now, you may know that toxic parenting runs through your family tree like capricious branches. You, however, want to break away and do things differently. You are exhausted about the patterns of toxicity and negativity that underlie your relationship with your children, and you'd give anything to stop the arguments and build a healthy bond with them.

I know, from first-hand experience, how difficult this can be. It's hard knowing you want the little ones to understand you want the best for them, especially when showing them what's right and doing so with kindness. As a parent myself, there have been so many times I've wished for someone to give me a solution. And, from what I've seen of life, it thrives when surprising you, particularly in the oddest moments. You never know when you will chance upon something that will change your life forever.

For me, this moment came when I heard the words "gentle parenting" for the first time. The juxtaposition made me curious— could it really work? From there, I spent years researching and delving deeper into what makes us tick as individuals and parents. Today, I am here to give you everything I have acquired in theory and practical experience. This book is a labor of love, not because of what I aspire to share with you, but because *I've seen the world of good it can lead to.* My children have grown up into some of the most wholesome people I've been blessed to be around, and this, in itself, is testimony to the power of the quiet strength you will soon acquire.

Together, we will:

- Discuss strategies to improve your relationship with your children and break away from toxic generational cycles. You will also learn practical communication tools that will make parenting more of a journey and less of a war.

- Understand the role our lineage and descent play in how we are conditioned to parent and identify emotional management so we may confront our weaknesses.
- Replace unhealthy coping mechanisms with healthy ones, so we become equipped to differentiate between punishment and discipline.
- Comprehend that discipline is essential, but it can be dealt out in compassionate ways to foster a home built on radical love and much more!

We may either instill in our children a fear of punishment and a yearning for compensation that makes them feel inadequate. Or, we can educate them to respect those in authority and do the right thing because they deserve it. The issue goes beyond just toeing the line. It's about being kind, friendly, attentive, and a well-rounded person. A child's ability to comfortably adjust to their surroundings is a critical factor in how well they will perform in school compared to socially awkward peers. Disciplining kids isn't just about getting them through childhood; it's about influencing their whole lives. Let's work together to figure out how to raise well-adjusted kids who will go on to be good people.

One chapter at a time. Come, let us begin.

Chapter 1

Understanding Your Family Lineage

"We are linked by blood, and blood is memory without language."

Joyce Carol Oates.

The mannerisms defining our parenting styles are influenced by a number of factors, including genetics, social support, financial resources, the larger environment, and our temperaments. While considering all these determinants, we may forget to look at the most important among them— parenting. Connection is the foundation that has helped humankind survive for as long as it has. Knowledge of our family histories can serve as a roadmap to help us understand and identify common patterns in how we parent our children.

Conscious awareness, in turn, creates an environment where it becomes possible for us to know what mistakes our parents may have made and how they contributed to our feeling lost, left out, insecure, or afraid while we were growing

1

up. So, if you've caught your words in the middle of speaking to your child with an alarming thought along the lines of, "Oh my gosh, I sound just like my mother!" you are not alone. It's only natural that the person or people we rely the most upon for our very survival should leave the greatest impact on us later in life.

Your Family History

I'll go over the two practical aspects first. Awareness of your family history gives you a deep insight into your cultural background, which is something that helps you build a strong sense of who you truly are. The ways in which you relate to your family, to create and extend your self-narrative, eventually give birth to your authentic and unique core identity. In turn, your children will have a natural curiosity about their background. Knowing where their roots lie will not only increase their self-respect, but also allow them to view the world beyond the narrowness of bigotry and limited cultural perceptions.

Secondly, you should know your family history so you have an accurate rundown of any illnesses or health issues that may be genetic. A complete health record would cover information spanning three generations, including siblings, parents, cousins, grandparents, and children. Our families bear similar genetic backgrounds and often live in the same environments and experience mirroring lifestyles. When taken together, these factors can help you become aware of different health conditions that could run in your family. If you can't have everything, do the best you can.

However, these are not the only, perhaps, not even the most important, reasons why you should have good knowledge of where you come from. In my book, your history and understanding why you responded in specific ways during your childhood, gives you the ability to either repeat or reject the patterns you went through. The health and happiness of your children are formed around this.

Experiences garnered in our early childhood, and the interactions we have based on these experiences, give us our earliest comprehension of emotions and how we should or shouldn't express them. The attachment theory, for instance, discerns that we develop a good idea of how relationships work at the end of our first birthday. At this point, the only sources for this idea are the ways in which our parents and primary caregivers responded to our needs.

The issue arises when our early experiences regarding parenthood are not as pleasant as they could have been. The quality of our early attachments profoundly impacts how we behave as grown-ups. A child is secure and takes comfort in their established attachment forms when their expectations surrounding comfort, shelter, and relief from stress are met appropriately and in a timely fashion. A child who is confident in attachment patterns will be freer to explore and learn, therefore subjecting their mind to optimal development as well as experiencing better emotional well-being than one who is insecure and frightened. Essentially, we internalize a model (unconsciously) that tells us what the "correct" way to parent is.

Dan Siegel, a noted child psychiatrist, believes that we all have the power to rise above our childhood experiences and develop healthy, loving relationships with our children. Based on his research, he postulates that what is more important than what happened to you as a child, is *how you make sense of* the way those experiences have influenced you. From there, you can use that knowledge to better parent your own children, (Siegel & Hartzell, 2013).

A difficult childhood, while painful and testing, doesn't necessarily mean you will recreate the same negative patterns with your own children. I speak from experience, for I come from a background where parenting was rigid and often involved less-than-ideal forms of discipline. What I have known is that people are not always able to account for their emotional resilience, and sometimes, they act in ways they normally wouldn't if they were in calmer mind frames. So, when we do resort to age-old patterns that we believe are ingrained in us, there is a high possibility we're frustrated, angry, and not in the space of mind to think consciously about what we are doing.

We begin acting on autopilot and do whatever comes naturally to us, which, of course, can be a mistake when we are raising whole other human beings. It takes an immense amount of self-evaluation to break away from the negative patterns of family interactions that may be handed from one generation to the next. However, once you become a parent, you kind of know this is one sacrifice that's worth making. Parenthood gives you the opportunity to grow with your children and engage in intimate, healthy ways of raising them. It's not easy, but you are free to choose which behaviors will support your child's overall well-being and let them feel safe, loved, and competent. The first step, of course, is awareness of your patterns and their origins, which is why knowing your lineage is so important.

The Centers for Disease Control and Prevention (CDC) tells us that while our brains continue to change and develop as we transition into adulthood, the first eight years of a child's life remain the basis for their future learnings, health, and life-long perceptions of balance and success (*Early Brain Development and Health*, 2022). Early childhood is a key phase for your child's emotional and mental growth, and what they perceive and experience will inevitably shape their future. The future course of their health and well-being is hinged upon their childhood environments, the cues from these environments, and how they respond to them.

Poor Parenting Can Be Passed Down Through Generations

Over the years, many of us have become adept at pushing things so far down under that we forget they ever existed. It wasn't so long ago that corporal punishment bore quite a bit of legitimacy as an acceptable way to regulate children. Public opinion may have worked— at least in theory— with the notion of corporal punishment being deemed unethical, but is it really all gone? I wouldn't be surprised if the practice is still as entrenched as it was a decade back, even if it is done in more secretive, clandestine ways. As recently as the 1980s, spanking, as a threat, was just another subtle norm entrenched in American households, practiced but never spoken out loud. It was always a way to keep children in their place. In 2013, for instance, a Harris Poll discovered that 81% of parents believed hitting (specifically, a "good, hard spanking") to be an acceptable way of disciplining children, and two-thirds even said they had used it as a means to instill obedience, (Cuddy & Reeves, 2014).

We're also quite familiar with the tongue-lashing and the slew of angry, disappointed abuses that would follow in the wake of a half-completed or poorly-done chore. We learned to think it was better than getting hit with a belt or having flying slippers tossed at us with Olympic precision. Verbal tirades somehow escaped the "abuse" label, but not anymore. Again and again, studies have proven harsh physical *and* vocal punishments are not just harmful and useless; they can also ignite severe, lasting physical and behavioral deformities that accompany children well into adulthood.

With all the overwhelming evidence that keeps pointing to our need to step away from forms of abuse as we seek to instill discipline and responsibility in our children, I can only ask—

why do substantial chunks of the populace still seek recourse in vituperating against the very beings we love so hard and so much? Turns out there's a reason for that too. In a study published in 2010 by the Social Development Research Group (University of Washington), adults who endured forms of abuse as children may repeat these patterns with their offspring (Bailey et al., 2009). Poor parenting, which usually includes one or multiple forms of abuse, was common across three generations, suggesting that the choices we make as parents can run in our families longer than we'd think. Susan Newman, a social psychologist, notes that breaking away from the cycle is a lot like breaking a difficult, addicting habit, because you come to identify it as something to rely on (Newman, 2003). It becomes your conduit to expressing the rage and frustration you've built within you all these years, and if you can't embody what you've been taught, you naturally begin feeling restless and inadequate— even if the changes you're making will bring a lifetime of good.

A news report published by NBC (National Broadcasting Company) in 2016, reported the offspring of parents with difficult childhoods are six times likelier to demonstrate emotional and social problems (Fox, 2016). The report covered the work done by a group of researchers who studied the entrenched, prejudicial thought patterns that formed the basis of parenting choices. The designs included wrong assumptions, like picking up a screaming baby would spoil them or believing that boys who cried were intrinsically weak and "girly." There was also the notion that a young boy was supposed to take a truant father's place as the man of the house, and one that reported failure to comply with rules could only be dealt with an iron fist.

The researchers also came across beliefs that children who were teething and bit others should be bitten to show them what it felt like, or children could only be made to behave by being spanked. It doesn't take a scientist, but it does take convincing some very stubborn folks— to know that spanking won't accomplish what they hope it will and can, in fact, be pretty aversive for children in the long run. Researchers like Elizabeth Gershoff have long noted spanking isn't related to compliance and can lead to social, behavioral, and cognitive maladaptations (Gershoff & Grogan-Kaylor, 2016). However, parenthood isn't supposed to be a breeze. It's a learning curve, and while it can be difficult for you to emerge out of the cycles perpetuated in your family's history, it's certainly doable. The first step begins with acknowledging and recognizing the face of abuse. The act of disciplining a child has cultural connotations, and while there will be variations depending on the "norms" of your society, look at the humane and objective ways first.

Now that you're an adult, you have the perspective to remove yourself from what you now see as hostile or damaging tendencies, enabling you to avoid passing them on to your children. Instead of trying to bury your feelings by adopting an "it doesn't matter; I came out alright" mentality, try to work through them. The feelings won't go away; instead, you'll seek more hurtful ways to subconsciously manifest them, including expecting your children to "suck it up." Consider a child getting shouted at for being naughty— what would be the initial thought in their heads? They wouldn't think of the long-term "I'll never do this again" solution. They'll be focused on the immediate objective— getting you to calm down, so you stop shouting and scaring them. They'll likely repeat what they've done and learn to hide it better. As someone who loves your child, you want to avoid this.

The Pitfalls Of Repetition

It is logical for us to want to imitate the positive episodes that characterized our childhood and youth, but, in the same breath, we must become aware of conscious parenting. When you aren't present and genuinely focused on the words leaving your mouth or the thoughts running through your mind, you may repeat the mistakes that run the "Am I a bad parent?" nightmares you have at night. In some cases, you may be repeating negative comments or the same actions you saw your parents do — which, while hurtful, got the job done. Imagine telling your child to "use their brains," when they can't get a math problem right. If you stopped to think, you might find this is something your parents used to say to get you to achieve something. If it hurt you, it's bound to hurt them too. Results born out of coercion are truly not worth losing the faith and adoration of your child.

Some of us also tend to overcompensate for what we perceive as failures in how our parents raised us. If we didn't have a lot of money growing up, for instance, we could find it easy to give in and buy your children mindlessly expensive gifts because you don't want them to experience a hankering for something and never getting it. Gentle parenting doesn't ask you to spend big bucks on your kids and win their affection with over-the-top baubles. Rather, it asks that you reason with yourself and understand why you're spending so much on them, and to look for solutions that will enhance and nourish your relationship beyond the boundaries of all that is superficial. There is a line between sufficient and far too much. Overcompensating because of your history makes it blurry. When we overdo, we attribute to our children the feelings, wants, or characteristics we had when we were young. Consider a hypothetical scenario— you repeatedly enquire about your child's social life at school. You worry as to whether or not they are successfully forming friendships. The root cause may not have anything to do with their social skills, but can rise from the fact that you had a hard time making friends when you were younger.

As a parent repeating the wrong patterns, you could find yourself unconsciously recreating situations that you experienced growing up. Perhaps you never talked openly about the problems you faced, either as a child or a complete family. Maybe you watched your parents lie to you, although you knew the reality was different. Once you start your family, your thought process may mistake you into thinking what your parents did made more sense since they were trying to protect you. However, introspection and discussion to arrive at constructive solutions as a family is always better than keeping things buried. Children usually get wind of what's going on, because, well... they love you. They love you and they know you more than you'd think. The idea that something is going on with the people they care so much about— something they can't help with because you don't find them ready or important (they won't understand the more mature reasoning) will do nothing but hurt them.

Parenthood involves choices and decisions. Many adults refuse to consider accepting help or going to therapy because they think it shows their weaknesses. The reasoning behind this usually dates back to when they are children, and their parents tell them that the world has no room for people who display their vulnerabilities or talk about their issues. Later on, we also teach our children the same thing, even if we feel it's important for them to ask for help when they need it. We forget they are upset and anxious about something that may not seem significant to us, but is very important to their little minds and hearts. So, a key step in the road to progress lies in identifying our triggers and knowing that asking for help does not make us weak. There is a silver lining. You are not destined to be determined only by your heredity. You have a conscious, independent mind that can renew itself and form new habits. After all, you know your child(ren) best, and your understanding goes far beyond the patterns that have characterized your youth.

Heredity Beyond Physical Traits

The process through which genetic material is handed down from parent to offspring is referred to as inheritance. Tangentially, people who come from the same family have a predisposition to share comparable features. If you find you have something in common with your parents, siblings or other relatives— such as eye shape and color, build, hair consistency, facial features, and so forth, it is because you have inherited the same physical traits that run in other members of your family. However, inheritance is not limited to the mere physicality of your features. Seemingly, parents stand to hand down the ways in which they think, speak, and act.

A study conducted by two psychologists from the Michigan State University looked at a popular theory claiming the manner in which parents run their households (and manage their children) are strict consequences of what they have internalized from their parents during their childhoods. The researchers found that, interestingly, both environmental factors and a person's chromosomal makeup (that is, their genes) played important roles in parenting (Klahr & Burt, 2014). The way in which a child is raised is not the mere function of how their parents were treated as children— there are also genetic influences involved. They conducted a statistical analysis spanning fifty-six studies the world over, each focusing on the origins of parenting behaviors.

The results revealed genetic influences in parents determine 23-40% of nurturing traits, including parental warmth, negativity, and forms of control. Importantly, the researchers also made note of something that really struck a chord with me — the children's characteristics play a very dominant role in shaping all aspects related to how their parents treat them (Klahr & Burt, 2014). I'd say this works in a cycle. If you raise your kids to be sweet and warm, your parenting will grow mellow and more wholesome over time. If, however, your kids are rebellious and discredit you at every step, implementing softer styles pertinent to raising them becomes challenging. The sooner you make it a priority to wield discipline in a manner that instills both respect and conscious understanding in them, the better for everyone concerned.

Do Hereditary Behaviors Exist?

The inheritance of physical traits is something that you can literally see or experience with your own eyes. When you see parents and their children together, it's not uncommon to note they have the same eye color, for instance. However, behavior is a whole other genre and a more complicated one, at that. It involves a complex interaction between the environment and your genetics. You can be a beautiful dancer, and perhaps your mother was also a renowned dancer in her youth. But, is your talent genetic, or is it the result of years of training from when you were four years old? Maybe you were born with two left feet, but the time you've spent practicing has wired your brain to just know which steps flow and which don't. The thing is, you're not inheriting behavior, per se. What's getting handed down are the *genes*. Genes comprise information that generate proteins which can come together in many different combinations. Each of them affect our behavior. Even so, there's the environmental bias— because not all genes function the same way.

Have you heard of *epigenetics* before? My first understanding of the term took fruition when I began my research for this book. Epigenetics examines the ways in which one's actions and surroundings may modify one's genetic blueprint. Epigenetic alterations influence how the body interprets a DNA sequence, but do not permanently alter the DNA sequence itself, making them reversible in contrast to genetic changes. The lived experience of every breathing organism, therefore, has the potential to impact their gene's behaviors. In addition to epigenetics, another ongoing debate across different health fields is that of 'nature versus nurture.' The underlying question remains the same— which behaviors are learned, and which are inherited?

The issue that plagues our understanding is character traits, unlike physical traits, can be passed down both through genetics and upbringing. You can't inherit blue eyes because of your upbringing, but you sure can be burdened with a terrible temper, if that's what you grew up around. Similarly, if you were brought up by economical parents, there's a strong possibility you could grow up to be cautious and frugal with your money. If, on the other hand, you grow up in a home that spends lavishly without much afterthought, that becomes ingrained in your mind as something that's just done. Throughout different points in history, this nature versus nurture argument has adopted different forms, sometimes to extreme levels.

What most won't tell you is the subjective nature of your behavioral inheritances. Yes, you grow up exposed to a specific pattern of behaviors. But it isn't unheard of to see children who are the polar opposites of their parents. I'll refer to a film I love dearly and always turn to for comfort— *Confessions Of A*

Shopaholic, where Isla Fisher plays the role of a bubbly Rebecca Bloomwood. Rebecca is pretty much the antithesis of her ultra-frugal parents (she's actually a raging shopaholic). And, while this is only one fictional example, we've all known people who've rebelled against the character traits imposed on them during their childhood and become the very opposite of what was expected.

Moving forward, here's what you need to remember:

- Nature and nurture don't work in polar opposites. Rather, they function together to build and hone the people we eventually become.
- Both nature and nurture are factors that influence human development.
- The environment in which we are raised triggers expressions of behavior, irrespective of genetic predispositions. Genetically identical people— say, siblings, if exposed to different learning environments, can grow up to be two completely different people.

Studying Your Personal Tendencies

Personality is one of the foundational basics underlining how we differ from each other. If we observe people around us, we'll be amused at how different and similar people can be from each other— pretty much in the same breath. Some talk incessantly, while others are reclusive. Some are active, while others prefer to lounge and be at rest. Some worry like it's routine, and others take everything in their stride. Every time we associate an adjective with someone— "talkative," "quiet," "reticent," "anxious," "easy-going," "lazy," "hyperactive," and so on, we're talking about a core trait that defines their *personality*.

The best way to understand the differences between two individuals is to look at their personality traits or personal tendencies. These traits/tendencies highlight the basic dimensions that make people distinct from each other. Every person falls on a particular spectrum on each dimension, meaning they could be high, low, or medium, concerning the extent to which they exhibit certain traits. If, for example, the measurement is "impulsivity," person A could score high, B medium, and C low. This would mark the differences in their personal traits regarding their impulsiveness.

The FFM (Five Factor Model) was proposed in 1992 by Costa & McRae to understand the relationship between an individual's personality and behaviors. In broad terms, it is a model comprising five parameters to describe someone's personal tendencies. They are known as the *Big Five* factors, which is why the model is often termed the *Five Factor Model* (Soto & Jackson, 2013).

- The first component of the model is *an openness to different experiences.* Those who score high on this dimension tend to be very active individuals who are tremendously inclined toward aesthetic appeal and creative pursuits and prefer their hearts over their heads when it comes to decision-making. They are usually open to learning new skill sets and seeking exciting experiences.

People who are open to new learnings can be very broad-minded and have a modern outlook on life. Conversely, those who score low on this parameter would be more conservative, unwilling to consider changes, and in favor of a more traditional way of living.

- The next component is conscientiousness. This is, essentially, a measure of morals. The conscientious will fall back on compunction and possess a strong ethical and moral code. They will be self-disciplined, upstanding, and cautious about their public image (at least in terms of being lawful and moral citizens). They will think twice before acting upon anything. They can be perfectionists and seek methodical precision in what they work on.

People scoring high on the conscientiousness scale are goal-oriented, meticulous, and proactive. They work hard to achieve their objectives in given time frames. Those who are at the other end of the scale are more laid back, not as goal-oriented, and willing to go with the flow.

- Then we have extraversion and introversion. We're likely quite familiar with both terms since they've attracted the fascination of so many millennials. We refer to an extrovert as one who is more concerned with being the life of the party. They're always seeking the limelight, always talking with others, boisterous, confident, and at times loud. They abhor spending too much time alone and prefer being the center of attention.

Introverts are those who revel in the solitary pleasures of me-time. They are generally recluses who have a very close circle of friends. There's a trendy saying doing the rounds— it goes something along the lines of introverts make friends by getting adopted by extroverts. But, fun and games aside, introversion is a state of being where one is content being at home rather than cruising outdoors. They speak less and enjoy being in their own company.

- After extroversion and introversion is trait four—agreeableness. It's pretty self-explanatory, but agreeable individuals tend to be very accommodating. They don't complain about unforeseen changes and accept that some surprises will always be unexpected as long as life exists. They're usually very open to helping others navigate through complex changes while also learning and growing with each experience that comes their way.

Conversely, those who score low on this trait can have difficulties adjusting to others and be averse to any changes. They may come across as afraid, even unfriendly.

- Finally, we have neuroticism. This trait highlights individuals who tend to hinge too much of their time on negative thoughts like envy, guilt and anger. Their proclivity toward negative emotions unfortunately creates fertile ground for mental health issues like depression. They can have a very hard time coping with stress.

The FFM, however, is not without its difficulties. What if our understanding of different personality traits are an illusion, and people refuse to conform with consistency in terms of situational variations? For instance, what if an introvert turns out to be very talkative when in a group comprising close friends? Would they still be an introvert within that circle, or would they suddenly become an ambivert or extrovert? In 1968,

Walter Mischel published *Personality and Assessment,* a book that questioned the very basis of personality psychology (Diener et al., 2021). He suggested that if you were to look at human behavioral tendencies across different situations, you'd be surprised at the lack of consistency. Children who cheat on some tests, for example, may meticulously follow rules while playing games and never tell any other lie— they may simply cheat because they're afraid of not doing well, and not because they are characteristically dishonest. Therein arose the human-situation debate, which pits our personalities against situational factors as core determinants of how we behave in different social settings.

Which route would you take, then? How would you understand what personal tendency truly speaks of your nature— especially now that you've been told you could be a raging parent under some situational circumstances, and a doting nurturer in others? Which one is relevant? Well, first of all, take a deep breath. This can be pretty overwhelming at the onset, but the answer is simpler than you'd think. Look at this paragraph once again. The one common determinant through it is the *situation.* So, to know your specific behavioral tendencies, reflect on the situation that is eliciting a particular reaction from you. Each such circumstance will make you evaluate the risks and rewards present in the very moment depending on *how you act.* So, if the circumstance is one where you must scold your child to get them to understand something (which is your reward) and this outweighs the risk (which is them being upset), you display anger. Simultaneously, if the risk is far greater than the reward, you exercise caution and put your point across in gentler ways. The important predictor here is **your perception of the risk and the reward pertinent to the situation.** That will tell you what your primary behavioral tendency is.

Benefits Of Knowing Your History

Now that you know the various nuances surrounding your personality and the means to verify your behavioral tendencies, you may wonder if it is really necessary to know your family history— going beyond the fact that you may influence how you raise your kids based on what you have learned in your childhood. Of course, the most obvious benefit is that knowing your ancestral history will give you an account of any medical issues that may run in the family.

There's more, though. Awareness of your roots will help you understand where you have come from, and give context to your life. When you start knowing your family history, you could learn about new members of your family— ones you weren't familiar with before. Years back, I saw a documentary of a Holocaust survivor who thought his entire family had perished during the war. He studied his family lineage and found he had a nephew who was well and alive. Imagine thinking your entire lineage is reduced to cinder and smoke— only to find that it is still alive, still present, waiting for you to find it.

Knowledge of a strong family narrative has a very positive effect upon your emotional health. Researchers from Emory University performed an experiment where they asked forty-eight families twenty questions about their lineage. They discovered that the more children knew about their families, the stronger their sense of control was. They also had more self-esteem and were certain they came from functional, successful families with strong, stable dynamics (Clark & Kurylo, 2010). Knowing their ancestral history gave the children a sense of integration and connection with resilience. It allowed them to see how rooted their identities were, for even at the tender age of nine, they understood they came from a tree rooted a hundred years back (Fivush et al., 2010). All of us like to know we've come from something momentous. What better way to find out than by studying and reveling in our ancestor's lives and pursuits?

Knowledge of our family history can increase compassion. Knowing where we come from can help us understand our place in the world, and in tandem, we also learn to respect the spaces that belong to others. Seeing how your forebears and distant relatives observed holidays may be a fantastic experience. You may broaden your views and deepen your comprehension of your own convictions by learning about the experiences of people who are not like you, in terms of religion or cultural backgrounds. We become more aware of life's inevitable ups and downs. For instance, one of my friends (who lives in another country) would often speak of how her grandparents migrated to their hometown following the Great Depression. What she learned grounded her and developed an immense sense of respect in her, regarding money and finances. She went on to ingrain the same kind of respect in her children. All of us gather stories because we hope, one day, we will be able to share them with our offspring. Knowing where you come from is a sure way of building a whole treasure-trove of stories to share.

In this chapter, we covered aspects related to understanding your family lineage, and comprehending how that lineage relates to your personal tendencies and the ways in which you may parent. Some aspects of our histories, however, may be rooted in toxic generational cycles. It is important for us to know them so we don't perpetuate their existence through our own offspring. In the next chapter, we will get to the core of understanding these cycles and how they may impact your parenting.

Chapter 2

Toxic Generation Cycles: How They Affect You And Your Kids

"I deeply believe the work of breaking our inter-generational patterns and cycles is an act of love."

Gwynn Raimondi.

You are the creation of generations of stories and struggles. At the heart of this idea lies the word "generation." For purposes of building a stable narrative, I will now make use of a hypothetical person called Amie. Amie's parents doted on her, and they wanted only good things to illuminate her future. Yet, when she was of age, Amie began acting out in strange, unwarranted ways. The situation got so bad that she eventually landed on the receiving end of a therapist's table. From there, months of groundwork revealed Amie had developed deep-seated generational trauma. Her mother, completely unwittingly, had spent most of Amie's childhood telling her (in entirely unconscious ways) that she had to be good if she wanted society's appreciation, including the love of those who mattered the most to her. For years, Amie sought to live up to that impossible expectation.

Amie kept straight A's, excelled at sports, maintained a demure persona, and true enough, everyone found her to be the "model kid." But no one asked if there was any pressure from the inside, causing all of her defenses to crumble one-by-one. The last straw came when she found one of her friends being loved by her family irrespective of how naughty she was. An immediate sense of unworthiness ate at her— and then, things fell apart until she couldn't take it any longer. Generational trauma can be the unspoken, unseen, yet perennially present monster under our beds. We don't understand what it is, and what damage it can inflict— sometimes, not until it is quite late and a lot of damage has already been done. Fortunately, in this chapter, we will try to establish a concrete understanding of the concept and what it entails, with the hope that knowing what it can do will give you the essential information you need to deal with, and rise above it.

Understanding Generational Trauma And Toxic Generational Cycles

To begin breaking generational trauma and toxic patterns, you need to know what they are. Let me illustrate this for you. Once again, I'll build a narrative surrounding Amie. Let's say that while Amie's parents loved her, they did not wish to be married to one another. They had come to a point where they found each other's company dull and uninteresting. The father dealt with it by being away from home as much as possible. The mother would get drunk and keep reinforcing the need for her children (Amie and Amie's brother) to be perfect so they wouldn't need to rely on another person. Whenever they were together under the same roof, there would be incessant quarrels. They refused to leave the dead marriage because they thought sticking together for the kids would be better— although by the time she was a teenager, Amie had come to believe differently.

They'd have the same fights, repeating themselves like a broken recorder. Some of these fights would involve her mother engaging in self-harm. The damage she and her brother received wasn't physical so much as emotional. They never learned how to love someone in wholesome ways, and without each other, they'd have come to believe that families were screwed up institutions which forced incompatible people to suffer together till the end of time. That would have become their toxic generational cycle. Amie found that she was attracted to partners who were abusive, for she sought to prove her worthiness to each of them. She developed a very misconstrued, broken understanding of what love was. Over time, and with enough therapy, she broke the cycle of abuse (as did her brother) but it took years. The lessons left scars, yes, but they also served as valuable reminders of what love should be, and what it most definitely was not.

At the onset, let's look at what trauma refers to from the perspective of mental health. It is an experience in an individual's life that leads to grievous harm that could be manifested in mental, physical, or emotional outlets. It creates a deep disturbance in the impacted individual's functional patterns and can often lead to feelings of helplessness and isolation. Trauma can result from big losses or events such as the passing of someone who is very, very close to the impacted individual. Trauma can also result from more innocuous patterns, like falling down and injuring a knee. In some cases, they can be a mix and merge of both. Situations of trauma that we may have read about, heard of, or experienced, include losing a loved one, dealing with the aftermath of a natural disaster, substance misuse or being in association with a person who abuses a form of substance, severe injury and illness, and witnessing violence.

When we encounter trauma, we experience emotional and physical reactions. Some manifestations include insomnia, anxiety, a sense of confusion and disconnectedness, recurring intrusive thought cycles, and complete or partial alienation from anyone who wants to help us. In children, trauma can be mirrored in psychosomatic demonstrations like stomach aches and fever. They may refuse to eat, throw temper tantrums, struggle with sleeping, cry when it's time to go to school, and display excessive patterns of attachment and attention-seeking behaviors. Generational trauma is a form of trauma transmitted through relationships built on attachment, where the parent has been impacted by relational trauma, which in turn impacts others across their lifespan and includes the proclivity to induce and spread further trauma (Isobel et al., 2018).

Of late, experts are trying to understand more about the impact of trauma on the human immunological system. They have found it can lead to immune dysfunctions, presenting in a hyperactive or malfunctioning system which bears greater receptiveness to autoimmune diseases and a general lack of immunity. Trauma also influences the brain's immune system, or the *microglia*. When someone is in a heightened state of trauma (and therefore, reactive) the microglia eat away at the endings of nerves instead of halting damage and enhancing growth. In essence, they go haywire and lead to anxiety, clinical depression and even dementia (Nahum et al., 2022). The rogue microglia can further contribute to genetic changes that get passed down through generations.

When a child's feeling of security and attachment within their family is repeatedly threatened, this is relational trauma. Both desertion and entanglement are typical causes of this disturbance. One or both of the child's parents or primary caretakers may be the root cause. Generational trauma, in bland terms, occurs when the psychological effects of relational trauma are transmitted from one generation to the next. Its onset may have begun decades prior to the current generation, but, much like humans being born, it has been handed down like an insidious heirloom no one asked for. It impacts how you understand, cope with, and heal from the pain of bearing the burden your ancestors cast on your shoulders. Your parents are not the creators of generational trauma alone. If anything, it may have existed long before their time. It could be that they witnessed the same at the hands of their parents, who witnessed the same with their caregivers. So it goes on until someone puts a stop to it.

Your body tends to remember what your mind may forget. So, with enough rooting, trauma becomes a part of how you respond without thinking. But this doesn't mean the mind ceases to exist. It's just not working consciously every time you fall into responding the way your trauma has taught you to. And this may be larger than the family. Races and demographics that have been subjected to systematic exploitation and repeated abuse, racism and abject poverty have all gone through trauma that has toughened them. While they became mentally tough, they also learned that the world has no place for those who are soft or emotional and so that is what they taught their children. Years back, a friend of mine who is African American told me his mother broke his arm and beat him multiple times because that's how *men were made*. History adds to trauma— and it goes beyond the narrative of one family to encapsulate entire communities.

Examples of Toxic Generational Cycles:

A generational legacy extends beyond the wealth you inherit from your forefathers. It includes perspectives, thoughts, cultural connotations, and beliefs that are passed down the family line. It is the lens through which you learn to see the world shaped by what your parents, grandparents, and other key influencers have taught you over many, many years. So, we pass on what we believe to be true and effective through our words, attitudes, behaviors and actions. And we think, subconsciously, even if some of these patterns are abusive and wrong, maybe that's how everyone does it. Maybe it's just a norm, a pill that you swallow because even if it tastes nasty, it's supposed to be good for you. Unfortunately, generational legacies continue like gifts that keep on giving, only stopping when you halt and say, "Enough. No more." Consider these patterns for a minute:

- Family One is emotionally numb. No one discusses feelings. It is an unspoken rule to pretend that everything and everyone is fine.
- Family Two considers discussing feelings or displaying vulnerability as a sign of weakness.
- Family Three has severe trust issues with accepting outsiders, which is why they reject all relationships their children form outside of the home.
- Family Four is overly protective and anxious that their children will make wrong friendships, so they homeschool them and limit their timings so they are back by six every night, although both children are almost young adults.

While not comprehensive on any accounts, this list is a reflection of how generational trauma and toxic cycles may present themselves in different families and carry from one generation to the next. You're not the first, and you certainly won't be the last person to think you don't want to turn out like your parents, even if you love them more than anything else in the world. You don't want to always worry about money. You don't desire a life plagued by constant quarrels with your significant other. You desire to be free from drinking as much as they do. You want a healthier relationship with your children. If you dig a little deeper as to what you don't like about the manner in which your parents treated you as a child, you may be shocked to find you are navigating life in the very same way— but you have been completely blind to it. Negative patterns may include, but aren't limited to outbursts of temper, domestic abuse and self-harm, gaslighting, lack of loyalty and fear of commitment, using children (unconsciously) as a means to drive your point home, and hostility toward your partner.

I return to Amie, who is now the mother of a five-year-old son. She thinks her son is a very anxious little cherub, and she also knows her mother and grandfather were plagued by anxiety their entire lives. Amie ends up believing that anxiety is a genetic issue that runs in her family. She's helpless against it, and eventually, she worries her son will grow up into an anxious adult because of the trait he has inherited. What she isn't actively acknowledging is that the anxiety may be existing because Amie, in utterly unconscious ways, has the same thoughts and fears that she is constantly projecting onto her son. She has the same thought patterns she grew up around, and if she keeps on this path, she will create an environment where her son is *exposed to anxiety* 24/7. Thoughts generate moods, and moods drive behaviors. So, the cycle is perpetuated.

It doesn't have to be, though. If Amie stops and decides to break the legacy of trauma by changing her thought patterns systematically, she will face exponential benefits (as will her son). If she learns to alter her fundamentally anxious thoughts, including the ones tied to worry and anxiety, her moods will also change, as will her behaviors, the manner in which she acts, and finally, how she treats her child. This requires immense self-awareness— but if not for her child, then who else for? She possesses the ability to help her son reframe his worries and fears and guide him into a different path of thinking, therefore breaking the toxic generational cycle once and for all. Yes, it's easier said than done. But, if it's worth it, it's doable.

The Workings Of Toxic Generational Cycles

Breaking a drawn-out cycle is a lot of work, but it can be monumental for the individual who is doing it, as well as the children they raise— and their future generations. If you are willing to raise your awareness and act differently than what you were raised to do, there are some patterns that need identification and interruption. Without further ado, let's dissect them one by one.

Emotional Parentification

Parents who conform to emotional parentification rely excessively on their children for fulfilling all their emotional needs and every lacuna they have in their lives. They expect their children to "man up" while their only business is playing and growing up, and require them to take, essentially, adult roles. This pattern's roots lies in the parent's emotional needs that were never fulfilled— either in their present lives, their childhood, or both. They may not be doing this consciously. Indeed, I've come across many parents who take pride in how "adult" their kids are, and how willingly they take up responsibilities they shouldn't have until they are of age. Unfortunately, the children become the targets of their parent's emotional hunger and fall at the receiving end of a continual tirade of demands. If anything isn't met, they may encounter dissatisfaction and disappointment from their parents, which they want to avoid at all costs. The pressure resulting therein limits a child's ability to focus on their emotional development. Here are some ways in which one may fall to this generational trauma cycle.

- Expecting a child to calm you when you are facing a difficult emotion.
- Seeking your child's attention, approval, and validation all the time.
- Making your child your confidant, hero, helper or surrogate spouse.
- Expecting your child to save you from your solitude, especially when they grow old and try to live their own lives.
- Expecting that your children will cater to the emotional needs of other family members when you don't want to.

Instead of falling into the pitfalls of one of the many traits listed above, here's what you could do instead.

- Understand the emotional void in your life and consider ways in which you can fulfill it without needing your child to address it. Their bond with you is different and everlasting, but it should not supplant your need for a parent or a spouse or a friend.
- Work on fulfilling relationships with a partner, other family members, or friends.

- Have different sources for meeting emotional needs, including hobbies, reading, art, work, spiritual pursuits, self-care, and personal growth endeavors.
- Keep a part of your identity distinct from your children and spend some time entirely on yourself.
- Practice self-love, self-regulation, and self-validation so your children don't need to love you because you need it, and they can instead love you *because they want to.*
- Develop a healthy understanding of your emotions and their management in relation to other family members.

Over Sheltering And Over Controlling

It's possible that your own traumatic experiences are the root cause of your desire to overprotect your children from the outside world. In effect, you are attempting to safeguard them from the same things that befell you. You will do all in your power to ensure the safety of your kid because you want them to live. On the other hand, providing an excessive amount of protection for your child might restrict the adventures they have throughout their lifetime. Or, it may serve as a barrier between you and your kid when they begin to investigate topics that you find controversial. Or, since your child has had no opportunity to independently evaluate risk, they can grow up to be frightened and avoidant of situations in which they might be put in danger.

The experience of trauma is often described as feeling as if one has lost all control over a terrible and potentially dangerous circumstance. The tendency to overcompensate as an adult by exercising excessive control is one way in which traumatic experiences in childhood might influence parenting methods. Children whose parents exercise excessive control over their lives run the risk of developing defiant attitudes or lacking the skills necessary for independent living. A significant number of people also acquire maladaptive habits, such as dietary illnesses or alcohol misuse, in trying to control their emotions.

Parental Projection

The process by which parents tend to put all their insecurities, fears, unresolved attachments and unfulfilled dreams on their children is parental projection. So, if you want your child to become a doctor or a lawyer because you couldn't be one, you're projecting your unrealized dreams upon them. You worry incessantly about your children and avoid turning inward to look at what needs to change— and more often than not, it is your own thought patterns. The impacted child may naturally feel trapped because they get robbed of the space in which they can be their own little selves, learn to function independently, and live their own unique dreams as they were meant. You forget that your child's life, while tied to your own, is distinct, and begin to look at your relationship as a parasitic amoebic mass that doesn't have any head or tail or limbs— it's just one blob of unified discontentment.

Here's a run-down of what projection may look like:

- You subconsciously use children to navigate through your unresolved issues about your own parents.
- You try to live vicariously through your children and expect them to fulfill all the fantasies that you did not get to experience in your life or career.

- You keep focusing on what's wrong in your children instead of looking inward to see where the root of all the wrongs is originating.
- You expect your children to become a mirror image of who you were and unconsciously compete with them, to the point of being partly angry or resentful when they succeed at something.
- You constantly feel as if your children owe you for the sacrifices you have made to raise them, and also partly resent them for what you lost out in life because you were too busy raising them.

Instead of projecting these unhelpful thoughts and behavior patterns onto your kids, here's what you can do instead.

- Acknowledge the presence of unresolved family and emotional issues with your parents and work through them, with your family if you can, and alone if you must.
- Keep learning and uncovering new parts of yourself without forcing your children to be what you could not.
- Process the core of your insecurities and fears— with a therapist if possible.
- Allow your children to develop their own voices, take risks, learn from failures, and experience their own emotions. Trust that they are resilient beings who will grow from their learnings.
- Celebrate all your children's successes, big or small.
- Understand your children have every right to become their own people and live their unique, unencumbered lives.

. . .

Neglecting Your Child's Emotional Needs

Parents who hold unresolved trauma tend to separate themselves emotionally from their children— to the point where they begin neglecting their emotional requirements. Your children are at an age where the validation and emotional support they get from their parents matters most of all. Parenting is supposed to make room for a space where your children and you are continually exposed to numerous vulnerable emotions, including guilt, sadness, anger, love, and fear. Unresolved trauma may prevent you from experiencing or allowing your children to process any of these emotions.

Children whose parents are emotionally distant may struggle to accept weakness or manage their own emotions as adults. It's usual for an avoidant to be clingy, demanding, or emotionally distant. Finding meaning in one's own life is a powerful predictor of one's parenting style, so it would help for you to work over the trauma you encountered as a child if you allow yourself to feel the anguish from that time. Consciously understand how it lives on in your adult memories, emotions, and relationships. As a parent, it's important to keep an eye on your gut reactions to certain scenarios. Do you want to be a parent in this manner, or are these just your first reactions? Or do you repeatedly engage in one of the trauma-based habits we discussed? The trick is learning to recognize these rhythms. You'll have a better grasp of what it is about your kids or the circumstances themselves that tend to set off your emotional klaxons and trigger harmful responses.

Trauma And Parenting

Unresolved childhood trauma tends to linger into adulthood, and if it continues unabetted, it manifests in our parenting styles. However, the difficulties we faced as children don't have to sound the death knell to our desires to raise our own offspring differently. We aren't destined to traumatize our kids or fall into an endless cycle of guilt because we know we are doing things that subconsciously hurt them. Children adjust to events the best that they can. But, emotionally traumatic experiences can make them more vulnerable to future trauma. If the emotions aren't processed at the time they are generated— either with the aid of a caregiver or through some form of support— they keep on building internally as forms of clustered trauma that can severely debilitate their ability to live healthy, wholesome lives.

In themselves, traumatic events spring forth impulses and emotions hinged on preservation of the self. When you process these happenings, you recognize what has happened and validate the emotions in the moment. This gives you a sense of safety within yourself— you are your own friend, projecting a safe space for you to talk about, feel, and express what has come to pass. Eventually, this kind of validation helps you rise above what has happened. You can come to a place of letting the pain go, and it will no longer linger as something that haunted you.

The kind of maturity you need to handle and process trauma isn't something you'd expect a child to have. Firstly, there's not enough support to enable the child to navigate through or make sense of what has happened. Emotions like sadness, anger and pain are very uncomfortable, and the child, in the throes of making sense of what has happened, may find it far easier to just suppress the negative tide and feign cheerfulness instead. Suppression is only useful for a day and a half, for sooner rather than later, the trauma will move into the child's unconscious mind, where it will linger, unresolved. A trauma that occurs in childhood, if left to fester, will be carried with the child as they become adults. Therefore, it isn't surprising for adults to find the root of their "adulting" issues has nothing to do with what happens to them in their later lives, but actually took shape years back, when they were only children. As a corollary, much of what you experienced in your childhood— depending on how (and if) you dealt with it, may influence how you parent today.

Some effects of childhood trauma can be as plain as a sunny day. It is those that are hidden that become all the more dangerous, because they have a way of sneaking into your daily life without notice. One day, you may wake up feeling absolutely fine. Then, you see your kid leaving crumbs on the table and immediately all hell breaks loose— not because you want to be harsh with them, but because you were always at the receiving end of physical and verbal bashings if you'd leave a dirty table after a meal in your childhood. You're not even thinking here— it just happens, like the twitch of an eye or a yawn. Trauma can, therefore, play a significant role in your perception of danger, the way in which you manage emotions, and how you respond to different stresses. Consider these instances. Do you:

- Experience recurring nightmares or unpleasant flashbacks?
- Have panic attacks and fears that occur without rhyme or reason?
- Think in black and white?
- Remain over-vigilant and in constant apprehension of threats, even if you are in a safe environment?
- Blame yourself all the time?

- Find yourself worthless?
- Suffer from eating disorders, self-harm and addiction?

Among the most apparent symptoms of traumatic experiences that have not been healed is avoidance. You may avoid, consciously or subconsciously, any sensations, memories, or circumstances that even tangentially bring up your prior traumatic experience. You may be able to steer clear of them by withdrawing from your child's life or by choosing to numb the sentiments via the use of substances or other maladaptive activities. You also have the option of restricting your child's involvement in events that you would prefer they not participate in. This may restrict their opportunities to participate in activities or experiences that they find enjoyable.

It's important to remember that no one chooses to experience trauma. To become a *better* parent, you must recognize how strong you have been— both in choosing to learn about what has happened, and in wanting a future where your children will be untouched by the negative patterns of your childhood experiences. If you can allow yourself to feel what you have suppressed all these years, and complete the cycle that got cut off because you couldn't deal with the pain of the emotions that arose, you will understand why the trauma hurt you the way it did, and *what you can do differently.* Emotional processing will help regulate your emotions, give you room to relate with and nurture your babies the way they deserve. So— what is the key? *Finding and facing your weaknesses.* We will discuss more about this in the next chapter.

Chapter 3

Facing Your Weaknesses

"Behind every young child who believes in themselves is a parent who believed first."

Matthew Jacobson.

Most of us begin something new with the intention of doing well. We become really excited at the onset, because we think the project we are embarking on signals a new phase in our lives— a grown-up, mature phase which will see us giving our best performances yet. Then, as happens with most things in life, hiccups come along. Whenever we love something, we will see parts of it that will test that love. We will encounter aspects of our adoration that seem unreasonable and unfair, and there will even be those tiny moments when we'll wonder if we're better off without any of it. But deep inside, we do know that the journey we are on is worth it, and perhaps, if we learned to look at the root cause of our problems by delving inside rather than looking at and blaming the external world, we'd find solutions that'd last us a lifetime. If you've looked at your kids after a really tough day of arguments and cross-countering and wondered, "Am I a bad parent?," know that you aren't alone. It's deviously easy to feel your parenting skills are subpar when everything is going south and your reservoir of patience is completely exhausted. Yet— and this is just a tiny sliver of silver lining— you're concerned enough to wonder if you're going wrong somewhere, and that itself is an indication that you're not a bad parent, you're just stuck in the weeds.

Sometimes, it may feel like every choice we make bears monumental weight, which means that every wrong decision will cause significant damage. If we scold our children because that seems like the better option, we spend sleepless nights resenting ourselves for having been too loud or too harsh. We worry incessantly about the long-term impacts of the routes we choose, especially when it's our children at the receiving end of the stick. We stress over a multitude of tiny worries that can become insidiously pervasive— were we too harsh when we scolded them earlier? Could we have handled their tantrum better? Maybe we were right? But, what if they got hurt? The real, bland truth is that *every* parent faces moments when the last phrase they want to hear is "you must be as cool as a cucumber." All of us make parenting choices that wouldn't sit well with our less-angry, more contained selves, particularly when we act when we are confused or frustrated.

Getting Stuck In Bad Parenting Habits

I sincerely believe most parents are just trying their hardest to be the warmest, kindest individuals they can be, even if their children are just having a field day of being really naughty. The definition of bad parenting doesn't limit poor choices to one act, rather, it looks at a series of miscalculations that can harm your child's demeanor and impact negatively on their cognitive development. You will likely feel guilty and be quick to reconcile, but the issue therein is that the damage may leave a subtle root that will eventually grow. Many of us also don't realize where we've gone wrong, since we acted on impulse when we were too busy, angry, or otherwise occupied. If the action is unintentional, we'll be likely to forget about it once it is over—but the children won't.

At the very onset, we will try a little exercise. It's called, "this is not my fault." Of course, you will use these words with caution, because if you have made a conscious error in judgment somewhere, it would serve you well to make amends. But, all of us have moments where we blame ourselves for something our children pick up along the way. More often than not, we make it a habit to think things like:

- It's my fault she's so unruly. I spoiled her too much and gave her more freedom than was necessary.
- It's my fault she's rude to her father. I didn't teach her good manners.
- It's my fault he scored low in the test. I should have worked harder with him.
- It's my fault he doesn't have any friends. I made him spend too much time at home.

Whenever you are on one of these guilt trips, take a minute to consciously think whether the thing you're blaming yourself for makes any sense. The real truth is that the guilt won't alter the course of life for you or your child. When you blame yourself, you're taking the added burden of your child's behavior on your shoulders instead of holding them accountable and showing them where they went wrong. The longer you blame yourself, the more you will resent parenthood, which will seem more burdensome than ever. Also, you don't want your child to think you'll take any and all responsibility for their behavior—because this isn't good for anyone involved. So, your child has to learn what they can do differently, and instead of spending time blaming yourself about what could have been, look for constructive ways to teach them how to approach situations differently. With this out of the way, let us now go through some of the unconscious manifestations of poor parenting choices.

Reprimanding Your Child for Speaking the Truth

Perhaps your child made a mistake, and was honest enough to come to you and tell you what they'd done. Instead of focusing on the good thing, which is the courage they have displayed in telling you where they went wrong, you immediately panic because they made a mistake, and begin scolding them. Now, I'm not saying you shouldn't make them understand where they went wrong, but in these situations, you could always begin with, "Firstly, I appreciate that you had the courage to come and tell me the truth. That's really brave of you. Now..." Show them their error, but also appreciate their honesty. It's a sign of how much and how hard they trust you.

Scolding Your Child In Front of Strangers

Your baby is being particularly unruly, and you have guests in the house. In an impatient fit, you end up in a screaming match in a house full of people they don't know. Children are highly sensitive, and many act out in crowded spaces, especially if they feel that their privacy is under threat. If you need to tell them off, either take them to another room or wait until your guests have left before speaking with them. Shouting at them in front of everyone will do nothing but hurt their already high-strung senses and make them feel you'd rather be around strangers than them. Remember, you're mature enough to know the world has other people, but they're at that age where *you are their whole world*.

Focusing On Advice Over Encouragement

Think of ways in which you can project something that is worrying you about your child so that it comes across as less of "you must do this" and more "I know you're capable of doing this." Whenever you feel tempted to say something that sounds like bland advice— for instance, "you should wake up early and study hard to do well!" encourage them with softer words that will leave an equal, and perhaps stronger impact. You could, for example, say, "you are so intelligent, all you need is a little more work. I can help you wake up early and smash this exam! We're in it together." The idea is to make the little one think you're on the same team, and that they don't need to be afraid of relying on you for help or support.

Unconscious Comparisons

Oh, but we've all been there. The last time I remember making an unconscious comparison was when my child was being a little hurricane, and unwittingly, I wondered for one brief minute— what if she would have been more like the neighbor's kid, who was always a quiet little cherub? The point is, we will have moments when we'll be tempted to draw parallels, because comparisons are part of human nature and also the means by which we improve ourselves. We don't just do it with our families or friends, we're almost always comparing ourselves against different yardsticks and wondering if we're good enough. When we give a conscious voice to these measurements, however, we risk our children feeling that we don't think they're good enough. This may be the furthest thought from our minds. But rushing to conclusions is something that's about as ingrained in us as yeast is to sourdough. Whenever you find your mind running to draw a parallel between your child and someone else, take a time-out and don't say anything out loud. Calm down, get your nerves in the right space, and come back to talk to your kid when you feel you can handle their emotions without getting your own thoughts fried.

Harmful Habits

We're living in the age of OTT (Over The Top) entertainment. Netflix, Disney Plus, Prime, Hulu— you name it, it's just one click and a few dollars away. Added to that, social media platforms like YouTube, Instagram and Facebook have added features like *shorts* which enables us to see small clips from the people we follow online, highlighting a few key moments of their day-to-day lives in video form. I don't need to tell you how addicting it is, but I'll illustrate. The first time I plopped my kid, then five years old, down with a smartphone open to YouTube, my only idea was to just keep her occupied while I sent an important email. I was so thrilled with the resonating silence that followed— she was entirely occupied, moving from clip to clip with ferocious concentration. From there, I made a habit out of keeping her occupied on social media videos from time-to-time while I got chores done. A week later, I wanted to spend some time with her after dinner. To my shock, she refused outright, and instead stuck out her little fists, demanding for the Ipad so she could cruise through YouTube shorts! That was when I realized I'd begun relying on technology a little too heavily.

So, in most families that do rely on granting screen-time to children, the idea is to carve out a little time for self-care, which is actually fine. Any routine that gets reinforced on a day-to-day basis will grow into a habit, and that's where you need to be careful. If you need some time off and use a social media platform or an OTT channel to distract your kid, do it with caution. And if the time has come when you must wean them from the artificial world of influencers and their unrealistic lives, make conscious choices. Find out what pushes you to hand over a phone to your child, and when you do give them access to the phone, move toward educational videos rather than the ones that scream mindless entertainment.

Of course, you will encounter some resistance when you ask your children to put the devices away and spend some time with you instead. If nothing else works, tell them you will watch something together, and consciously push towards making the activity more educational, or even just entirely wholesome. I loved watching Studio Ghibli films with my child, and I'd do that again in a single breath. And if you establish any expectations or rules around screen usage, make sure you are following them yourself. Finally, don't be afraid to be strict about the final rule— you are in charge, and if you must, take away the devices and turn your children to a new form of activity. It won't be long before they embrace a new habit.

Unleashing The Snack Monster

All of us love snacking on treats now and then, so when your child asks if you can take her to McDonald's after classes to get a happy meal, you go ahead and think she's earned it— it's only one happy meal, after all. She asks again a few days later, and now, you're a bit worried, but you'd like a burger yourself, so you play along. Soon, it becomes a once-every-four-days thing, which isn't good for you, and certainly not for your child. Many children also develop an unhealthy obsession with snack food items because they're left lying around the house without supervision. Some of us make the whole point of giving snacks a "reward" which can be entirely counterproductive. I found, to my shock, that the more I limited snacks by telling my kid she had to "earn" them, the more her penchant toward them grew.

Unconsciously, she developed an internal reward system that felt complete and satisfied whenever she'd munch on a bag of chips or nick a bar of chocolate from the refrigerator— because her mind had learned to associate the mere act of eating an unhealthy snack as a signal to release feel-good reward hormones. In the long run, this could be very danger-ous. A way out could be to encourage intuitive eating. You place a bit of everything on a child's plate— maybe baked, over-roasted crisps instead of the store-bought chips; a slab of choco-late, veggies, protein, and other carbs. Let them choose the order in which they'd like to eat. Chances are they will look at all food items as sustaining rather than obsessing over a select-few.

Unlearning Toxic Behaviors One Step At A Time

It's a generally accepted truth that removing toxic people from our lives works wonders for your mental health, although it may be quite difficult at the onset. Some of us even choose to forgive the ones who have proved wrong for us so we can move on in peace. However, what happens when the tables are turned and we end up being the ones who must forgive ourselves? What if the most toxic people in our lives are the reflections we see in our bedroom mirrors? No one likes to admit that we all have aspects we aren't proud of, but when we learn to let them go and forgive ourselves, we can move on and live lives that are happy, wholesome and content. If you have noticed toxic behavior in yourself, know you possess the ability to unlearn them. The first step is already done, because you're here, willing to take the first step. Recognizing your issues will bring you to the point of being ready to overcome them, so be proud of yourself because you're stronger than you know. Coming to peace with who you are and the journey you are on is realizing that your issues may have been a part of you, but not your entire identity. You aren't stuck with them for the rest of your life, and you have what is necessary to defeat them.

Recognize the triggers that compel you to act in certain ways. When we portray a particular emotion, more often than not, there is a root cause behind its occurrence. So, if your habit is ordering out for the family because you're too tired after work — look for the root cause, and how you can adjust your circumstances around it. Can you meal prep during the weekend so that you're covered for at least the first three days of the week? Even cut vegetables and fruit, if stored well, can make cooking for the kids an easier task.

Or, could you rely on the help of your partner to focus on more home-meals rather than the TV dinners of greasy, unhealthy food that isn't nutritionally composite for your family? The triggers, while compelling, are usually never as important as the reason to leave them. In this case, leaving the habit of relying on junk food for the betterment of your children is infinitely more important than just having it easy.

In the split second before you give in to your negative trigger, take a minute to pause and reflect. Make a mental note, "I will not indulge in this today." An assertive mindset is victorious against destructive routines because it leaves no opportunity for mental resistance. You may either repeat this to yourself mentally or aloud, whichever is most comfortable. Leaving the area and distracting yourself with another activity might also help you overcome the temptation to return to an unhealthy routine.

Always listen to what your children are saying. I can't stress this enough— because there are moments when all you want to do is give up and let them speak gibberish. It's true, you won't be able to make sense of what goes on in those little brains all the time, but you'd be surprised at how much they're willing to share when they are young. If you become attentive to their words and actions at this age, you reinforce that you are a safe space they can always turn to. If you've never been a good listener, perhaps the behavior stems from your childhood.

Maybe you always felt like you were being pushed over, or that there was no one to listen to you. That couldn't have been easy. So, don't let your child go through the feelings you experienced when you were being ignored. If you find yourself slipping off or are unable to hold your concentration, take a deep breath and count to three. Remind yourself that whatever your children are saying may be simple enough to you, but of insurmountable importance to them.

How To Stop Endless Reprimands

If you have developed the tendency to talk back to your child, now is the time to curb it for good. This often stems from our childhoods, when every argument we'd make would be met by a counter argument until we'd end up feeling invalidated. Of course the adult will be more reasonable. Of course they will know better. But the child is watching you and hearing your words. More often than not, they're going to take them at the upfront value— so if you make an angry face and yell at them, they're either going to yell back, resulting in a full-fledged power struggle. They could also react by withdrawing completely.

The entire scene could unfold as a domestic dance with the both of you getting stuck in harmful communication patterns. This isn't the same as physical fighting, of course, but fighting can take numerous forms— and becoming angry, shouting, repeating yourself compulsively— all point to distinct displays of anger, which constitutes one of the forms. As far as possible, if you're unable to stop an argument with gentle words, ask your children to take a time-out. Tell them to take some time with their thoughts, or, if they are young enough, sit them down and explain why causing a scene in the middle of a grocery aisle isn't the right way to go about things.

Here's a little secret. The fundamentals of gentle parenting is hinged on one core word. *Patience.* When you are unlearning toxic habits, you need to begin with small changes. Replace what you are doing in the moment if you feel like you are seconds away from indulging in a bad habit. Imagine your bad habit is getting worked up by your child's words and then getting into a fight with them.

The next time you hear them talk out of turn, begin with one gentle command along the lines of "we shouldn't act this way when we are in public." If they don't listen and begin screaming, before you react, pause for thirty seconds. Block it out. Block out the sound of their temper tantrum, block out the hurtful words. Only repeat one line in your mind's space for those thirty seconds. "I know better." Act only once this line has been reinforced, and do so with the conscious intention that you want to *stop the tantrum, not enhance it.*

In terms of disciplining children, the one rule to remember is that there is *no one rule.* One size doesn't fit all because all children have their own little quirks. So, what works on their sibling or on a friend's kid may not be suited to the kid you're trying to discipline. For some children, the same kind of discipline or guidance that has been tried and tested over and over again may not be the most effective. Keep in mind that kids, like grownups, have their own unique traits.

It's possible that one child is more prone to tantrums or stubbornness than the others. Experiment with a variety of methods so that you may adjust your methods of discipline to the specific needs of each kid. If one child can focus and stop dawdling around after a few gentle reminders, another may need tailored schedules, close supervision, charts and some further guidance before they are able to stick to a new routine. One child may correct their behavior after being warned about losing privileges, while another may need to have those things taken away. Do what suits your child's temperament and also doesn't need you to lose your temper.

Remember that gentle disciplining isn't the same as letting your children run lawlessly. You do need to teach them the value of good behavior because children who learn the value of good behavior will grow up contained, happy, and with clear knowledge of self-control. On the flip side, those who aren't given any limits and don't face consequences of bad behavior are spoiled, selfish, lack self-regulation, and are generally very unpleasant to be around.

Provide guidelines, boundaries, and firm, consistent punishments for misbehavior. Keep the broader picture in mind if you're concerned that disciplining your kid may make them resentful of you. A child's development suffers when they are not disciplined. As long as you respond to your child's transgression with love and solid guidance, they will learn and develop from their experiences.

As much as possible, *always follow whatever you want your children to do.* So, if you want your children to eat brussel sprouts, you will eat them too— it's as simple as that. I know they can taste pretty awful, the secret is to just find a way to make them palatable. Going on a slight bend here, brussel sprouts roasted with a dash of balsamic, honey and salt work wonders. Likewise, if you don't want your kid to fib, don't engage in word-smithing your way out of tricky situations.

Your children are going to emulate what they see, so if there's discord in the house, they will pick up on it. Their wee sensors will go off, and they will think it's okay to cause trouble because that's what they've seen you do. And no one likes it when a child's best comeback is, "that's what you did too!" It leaves us with little room to counter them. When you reprimand your child, always try to make it more of a learning endeavor where they see they're going wrong and they *can, instead, rely on you for a better example.*

Whenever you're disciplining your child, always keep firm limits and guidelines in place so they don't invite situations that call for punishment. Discipline is nothing more than setting boundaries for expectations so children learn what is anticipated of them. The main goal here is to build their confidence so they can regulate themselves, because when they learn they will also know that success is a marriage between hard work and discipline.

Rethink how you discipline them— your only goal here is to help them make good choices. If you can show them how to walk the right path in loving, constructive ways that focus on learning, not punishment, the cycle of toxic parenting will end with you. They will learn that there are new, gentler, and much more effective ways to raise kids— and this is what they will teach their own offspring in time.

With this, you now know that the kind of parenting you have accepted as "normal" in your youth isn't necessarily the kind your children have to get used to. If there's anything that tells me about the plethora of information available on some topics on the mysterious Web, it is that they wouldn't exist if there wasn't a possibility of overcoming the issue they're all addressing. In other words, if you do a simple search on "how to overcome toxic parenting cycles," you'll be bombarded with information on the Internet. This is because it is possible to overcome toxic parenting cycles, and so there are various solutions out there.

There is a solution, and in many different ways, all of them will guide you to the same route, one that is lit by patience and understanding that, while habits can be deceptively easy to fall back on, *you don't need to be defined by them.* You are your own person, a being with conscious thoughts, a spirit, and the ability to identify right from wrong. So long as you have the power to make choices, you also have the power to do what is right for your child and their happiness. Your emotions can be your worst enemy, but also your best friend in learning to lead by example. We will discuss more about this in the next chapter.

Chapter 4

Self-Work For Emotional Regulation And Management

"The golden rule of parenting is to always show your children the kind of person you want them to be."

Elizabeth Roxas.

P arenting a child is an intensely emotional pursuit, no matter how well it is done. It is a storm in a teapot, for at no other point in time will you experience so many torrential emotional manifestations within a singular relationship. There will be the simple, golden moments where you just revel in the innocence of their young company, enjoying the way their hair smells after a shampoo; cuddling or nuzzling against their warm, wrinkly skin; playing or laughing at their silly words and sounds; and learning to love the world anew through the wide innocence of their baby eyes.

There will also be times when your urge to protect them will be so fierce you'll want to shut off the rest of the world to keep them safe. Then, there will be challenges. Stress, frustration, anger at what you've had to give up, a feeling of failure when you hear them cry but can't seem to find the solution, and sheer hopelessness because, try as you may, their demands defy the very tenets of reason. In summation, you're on the most challenging, unforgiving, and rewarding roller coaster ride of your life.

You can't ride unless you've got proper seatbelts on, can you? In this case, the seatbelt is your ability to tune in and manage the tide of emotions before they overwhelm you and make you react out of turn. Every action and word you emit will make a difference in your child's development. Your responses will always have the ability to influence how they learn to cope, and what behaviors they mimic. Imagine a three-year-old falling apart because she cannot make sense of why you gave her her cereal in a green bowl instead of her usual orange bowl. It sounds ridiculous to us, but we're not toddlers, and their life is pretty limited to the world of bowls, spoons, and bibs at the onset. If you react with frustration and anger, or tell them you know better, you will only distress them further.

Before you can adjust their behaviors, you need to manage your own reactions. Learning begins with working on reducing your distresses, and then your child's. Take it as a given that these small things will pop up all the time from here on. You could either exhaust yourself and keep hurting your child, who really doesn't understand why you've changed the core of their whole world which, coincidentally, was an orange bowl. Or, you could just tell them something that'll spark their curiosity, and make a story out of changing bowls and why change is important. You may encourage your children to achieve academic success in their interactions with others, by modeling healthy emotional regulation for them via clear and compassionate responses.

Yes, managing negative emotions can be extremely hard because they are so strong and persuasive— they usually work a lot quicker than the positive ones as well. However, know that nothing worth having comes easy, especially when it concerns one of the most important relationships in your life, one that you will nourish, nurture, and prepare for a life that goes beyond you. The payoff here is huge, both for you and your offspring.

Always tune in and embrace the feelings coursing through you. If you are angry, don't start screaming, but also don't push it down. Stay silent for one minute, and let your mind do the talking. The mind, once again, will listen to you if you train it well enough. It knows what is right, helpful, and useful. So, think on these lines— "Okay, I'm angry. I recognize the emotion. My child is doing something that is irritating me. But, I know why she is doing it. She wants the old bowl. If I scream now, she will scream harder, and we will get nowhere. It's okay to be angry. I'm going to let the feeling pass through me before I open my mouth, not with anger, but with a solution."

How You Manage Your Emotions Can Affect Your Children

Emotions are neither good nor evil; they just exist. What you choose to do with your emotions determines whether they will be beneficial or harmful to you. What's most essential is that you check in and embrace your emotions in order to be able to make a deliberate choice, as opposed to a knee-jerk response, about how to respond in the most effective manner. If it feels far too much on some days, look at the behavior you are about to demonstrate in the context of your child, their temperament, and their overall development. This will help you form real expectations.

Expectations are important, because the meaning you give to your child's behaviors will reflect on how you manage your own emotions and the ways in which you react. If, for example, you see your kid's shouting as "manipulative" or "hurtful," you will react in ways that'll increase your emotional turmoil instead of calming yourself or your child. The reaction will be intense, which is never good because it shows your kid you don't have great coping skills. They won't stop the annoying behavior, but they will learn to conceal it better. Instead, it is far more likely that you will react calmly and productively if you approach your kid with empathy and see these actions in the perspective of natural growth.

You can't "make" your child do anything. What you have is control over how you respond to their actions, which in turn will show them the right ways to think, behave and act. So, everytime your child throws a tantrum and you plead with them to stop by promising you'll give them a cookie or some ice cream or an extra hour in front of television, they'll make one primary assessment— "tantrums work! Put that one down as a win, I'm absolutely doing it again!" Let's do a hypothetical scenario here. Three-year old Mary tells her mother, Amy, "You are the nastiest mom and I hate you!" after Amy tells Mary that her playdate is over and they must go home.

Our first step is tuning into our feelings. Amy is naturally angry, and she wants to hurl a stream of curses at Mary. She wants to tell her she's the most ungrateful child, and she has kept her entire day aside to get her to this stupid playdate, but it's never enough for her. Before she responds, she closes her eyes for ten seconds. She recognizes that reacting with spite will teach her child zilch, and only work to increase their distress, and the embarrassment of everyone else in the room. She takes three deep breaths and tells herself she'll unwind when her kid is asleep. Then, she focuses on how she can respond in a way that will teach Mary to manage her emotions and accept the boundaries that must be in place.

At this stage, it's time to look at the expectations of the child. Amy reminds herself that at the age of three, children are the objects of their emotions. Her goal, therefore, is to help Mary learn to cope with life's many disappointing dealings. She exercises restraint in her voice, and responds, saying, "I know you are sad that we have to go home. You had so much fun. It's always so difficult when a playdate ends. But that doesn't mean it won't happen again. And, I think you're strong enough to learn to be okay when things end, aren't you?" In one fell swoop, she tells Mary she has the confidence Mary can handle and overcome her difficult feelings. She's also sending a subtle message here— if Mary can't handle disappointment, she won't learn this skill.

The next step is to watch out for baits. Young children can be quite clever when it comes to it, and they will use whatever strategy they can to avoid doing what they don't want to. So, when Mary is saying, "you are nasty," she doesn't mean that her mother is really mean, she just wants to say something that'll divert attention and make her angry to a point where she'll be okay with leaving Mary at the house for a while longer while she storms off or acts out of anger. Instead, she takes her daughter home and moves to the next step, which is to set a limit and give choices.

She keeps her voice calm. "I know you don't want to hurt me, you are just having a tough time because you are upset. I'm going to give you two choices. You can come home and spend the night in your room, or you could come help me make dinner." If Mary can't pull herself together once they're home, Amy will move on to other work, showing her that she can tolerate her daughter's tantrums, and that she knows Mary has what it takes to calm herself. This leaves Mary with two choices— she can either waste more time being upset, or she can get on with her day. Mary is a child, and children usually choose the option that will get them the most benefit. If she notices that there is more to be gained from just moving on, that's what she will do. And, this will also give you a clear focus on how to parent without letting your child's whims get the better of you. It may be emotionally taxing at the onset.

Maybe leaving your child at their playmate's home for a few more hours would be the easier of two options. In the long run, however, if you show your child they can treat you however they want and get away with it because you'll give them whatever they desire, it won't be good— either for your kid, or your dynamic with them. As we grow, we learn that life won't always give us the things we desire on impulse. It helps if there are elders to ease us into understanding this and living with grace nonetheless. Dr. Claire Lerner, a specialist in child development and parent guidance, believes that a parent who has trouble regulating their own emotions stands to negatively influence a child. Poor self-regulation contributes to the child's already existing distress.

When parents show how stressed out they are, children inevitably feel the situation is larger and more troublesome. They enter a red-zone, where their minds and bodies may spiral out of control. In this situation, the only helpful thing is to get them back to a place of calm (Lerner, 2021). No lessons can be taught or imbibed if a child is flooded with an overload of negative emotions. In such moments, parents must exhibit that they are in control, and they can guide their children back to the light. In essence, children *must know they are safe and that their little, impossibly important worlds are not under threat.*

The impact of negative emotions also works as a two-way street. When a child throws tantrums because they're stressed, the parent who is already angry may find it harder to stay calm. Of course we love our kids and want them to feel great. When they don't, it's triggering because we don't want that for them. Seeing them in pain, or being near them when they express difficult emotions like frustration, disappointment and anger can elicit a knee-jerk reaction where we either overcompensate and give them whatever they want (regardless of how unreasonable it is), or minimize the gravity of the situation by saying something on the lines of, "it's nothing to be scared of!" Unfortunately, in the case of the latter, we may know there's nothing to be afraid of— *but they don't*. They need to witness that through your reactions. If you freak out while telling them to stay calm, it won't help. So, you need to be comfortable with knowing that your child will experience discomfort from time-to-time.

Does this mean you should avoid talking to them about their feelings? No, of course not. The feelings won't go away, irrespective of how irrational or difficult we might perceive them to be. The children will know you're avoiding the subject because of your reluctance to approach it, so they learn to hold back on their expressions. This is the beginning of a very counterproductive trait of bottling things in. Children forgo the healthy way which lies through emotional expression, and instead, keep pushing their emotions within until a time comes when they just burst forth in unhealthy, unsustainable ways. The only way is through *you*. This is the core of your parenting, and one of the biggest life lessons you will teach them. Help them manage and work through their emotions instead of unconsciously teaching them they are evil and need to be suppressed.

Dr. Lerner pertinently notes many of us become reactive when we misinterpret a child's behavior. Let's, hypothetically, say we come home after a long day of work and find our child has littered the whole living room with toys. Our foot immediately lands on a lego, and as we jump in pain, we scold our child harshly. Instead of saying sorry, they laugh and run off. Immediately, we think they're being avoidant and socially maladaptive and begin worrying our heads off. We worry we've raised them wrong and they may grow up taking pleasure in hurting others. The truth is that they're likely overwhelmed by our anger and disappointment. The angrier and harsher we get, the more their shame and desire to just get as far away from the situation as possible.

It's the same when we're in the middle of a grocery store and they throw a tantrum because we won't buy them an unhealthy snack. If we react with more anger, it's a surefire way to engage in a war of words or even earn a few well-aimed kicks to our shins (children can be surprisingly adept with their blows). Tuning in and managing your reactions can change everything here. Just letting them know, as calmly as possible, that they can continue embarrassing themselves as you check out would work better than fighting with them in a very public situation. Your way is to teach them to not give in to difficult demands, even if it comes from people closest to them. This is the lesson they will carry in future. So, before you react, take these points into account:

- When the parents of an out-of-control child stay loving, present, and calm, they are teaching the child to understand they are safe and secure no matter how big or small the impending danger may appear to their little hearts. The parents also display their ability to handle all of the child's emotions, that their child is seen and understood and accepted completely.
- The child of a calm, connected parent will always calm down quicker because they will look for ways to solve the issues at hand.

- When the parents don't overcompensate by giving the child whatever they want whenever they display anger or disappointment, they send the message that they believe their child is capable enough to make do with what they have, and that the child is clever enough to solve their own problems. Therefore, they build the child's confidence in their ability to master challenges.
- Finally, in managing and expressing their own emotions effectively, parents become powerful role models for their children.

Should You Hide Negative Emotions From Your Children?

Many of us worry that an unwarranted display of strong emotions will overwhelm our children. If you've grown up believing you should always talk about difficult emotions, or express anger and frustration when kids aren't around, you're not alone. We have the tendency to believe our children may "catch" the bad emotion and feel terrible. There's sound reasoning to this fear too— a study found that parents could transfer certain fears (in this case, fear of going to the dentist) to their children (Lara, Crego, and Romero-Maroto 2012). The other, very real trajectory, is that our children can stand to benefit from witnessing a parent who is real with them, who shows that everything isn't a bed of roses, and who can face difficult emotions, find solutions to the situations causing these emotions, and rise above them. If your child sees you being a champion to and of yourself, you naturally think they'd learn good coping skills that will serve them well in their later life.

So, what route should you choose?

Well, you should consider a few concepts when it comes to

displaying emotions in front of your children. These are suppression, uncontained outbursts of emotion, and conveying and communicating about emotions. The first is when you entirely hide all outward signs of whatever is going on within you. For obvious reasons, this is not healthy. It tells your kid you are emotionally unavailable and that emotions like anger, sadness, pain, jealousy, or fear (to name a few) shouldn't be displayed because they make you weak. It's also terrible for your overall mood, and can lead to lifestyle illnesses like high blood pressure and obesity. Research has also shown the act of withholding negative emotions (anger, resentment, and so forth) can lead to diminished relationship quality between parents and children (Le and Impett 2016). In other words, children feel uncomfortable around an unexpressive parent and usually always make repeated efforts to get the parent to interact with them.

Now, if you keep containing negative emotions, a time will come when you bring everything out in an uncontained outburst. Since it isn't balanced, it will be overwhelming in terms of intensity. You may say very hurtful things you don't truly mean, but you are beyond the point where your conscious thought and words are connected. In the moment, you cannot work on taking ownership of your emotions or regulating them, and later on, when you calm down, you may even have difficulty remembering half of what you said when you were angry. But naturally, the damage is done by then. Uncontained emotion, in the context of a phobia of the dentist, would imply behaving as if dental clinics really are scary places, rather than acknowledging the fear— "I am aware that I have a fear of this, and I am trying to find a way to deal with it."

Are You Letting Emotions Hurt Your Parenting Skills?

There will be times when your child's emotional reactions will overwhelm you. Things that they would have coped with better in the past may seem to be intensely difficult to deal with in the moment and leave you wondering why they aren't able to handle things as they normally would. In the heat of the immediate situation, we end up saying something like, "You hurt my feelings," or "I'm really disappointed in you." In effect, we increase the chaos that their little world is already experiencing, and of course, our own emotions are left the worse for it. They learn that our feelings are dependent on the way they think and act, and this is a responsibility that should figure in much later, not when a human being is five years old.

Dangers Of Not Managing Your Emotions As A Parent

Dr. Florence Huang, a well-known child psychologist, unequivocally feels that all children have one key trait— they love imitating their parents. They see their elders as role models and always tend to modulate their own behaviors based on what they are exposed to. As a parent, if you don't learn to channel negative emotions in a healthy way, your children may internalize how you act out without realizing it. In time, children express the stress they imbibe from you through background anger (Gonzales 2019).

Very young children— kids around or below the age of three— are complete newbies to the world of emotional regulation. If they witness emotional instability, they react in unstable ways. They cry frequently and become difficult to control, throw temper tantrums, and are overcome by anxiety and fear.

They may also become more clingy, refuse to eat, evade healthy sleeping patterns and develop phobias (Gonzales 2019). In extreme cases, when both parents are unpredictable and can't control their mood swings, the children may become emotionally unstable and traumatized, themselves. Growing up, these children are at high risk for developing anxiety disorders, depression, and personality issues.

Depending on their levels of development and age, impacted children display their burgeoning discomfort differently. Small children— including toddlers— may react by becoming overtly distressed and angry. Older schoolchildren may withdraw from their parents completely and retreat into their own worlds, often giving parents the wrong impression that they're doing "fine." When these situations are prolonged, the children's self-esteem is harmed. Feelings of shame and self-blame arise, and they feel humiliated, helpless, and most importantly, unsafe.

Controlling Your Anger

The wonderful thing about calmness is that when you get yourself under control, your children will also calm down. Calmness is as contagious as anxiety, which is why we feel so peaceful and happy when we are in the company of stable people. If you can't get calm and take control, you're building the same atmosphere for your child that you don't want them to experience. Let's say you're teaching your kid to swim. No matter how patient you try to be with them, they refuse to get the hang of it. Soon, they become whiny and cranky and begin talking back to you. You get more frustrated in the process and emotions like anger, anxiety, disappointment and guilt appear inside you. You blame yourself for being unable to teach your child something as basic as swimming. You've taken this responsibility on your shoulders, so it's unnerving that they just won't cooperate. Unhinged, you start screaming at your child. It gets worse because they become very anxious and can't concentrate. They're being pushed to do something they don't want to, and they fail on purpose.

So, whenever you feel stressed, instead of reacting and snapping, ask yourself, "How can I stay calm so I can actually help my child get to where they need to be?" Remind yourself you are not responsible to get them to swim, your responsibility is to be calm and *guide them*. You're teaching them the qualities — because swimming is something they'll get the hang of, later if not sooner. But once their personalities become defined by anger and resentment, there's no turning back. You don't want them to think you are out of control and that *they must change and behave properly to please you*. Your children don't exist for your sake. They exist as independent little beings who deserve to be shown the way. Nobody here intentionally loses it and gets all worked up. Yet it seems to occur spontaneously. Happily, you can learn to control your emotions and maintain composure.

Plead with yourself to do your best to maintain command going forward. Take note of the triggers—is it your kid ignoring you? Or do you find the inner anger demon raging because they keep talking back to you? Staying in control isn't easy, but you can make a commitment and work toward it. The first promise is to just not say anything, to not react at all when you feel anger arising. I'm not saying you can't express your emotions. I'm saying you should take a minute before you express them. Do what you need to so that you can be calm before reacting. I often respond by saying, "Give me a minute," and walk out of the room for a while. I don't *have* to react to my child. I will respond, but *when I am ready*. When our children disobey our requests, we feel frustrated. They refuse to hear us out or act in accordance with what's good for them in the long run— we know that, but they don't. The easiest way to handle it, in my opinion, is to just accept the fact that your kid is going to want to get under your skin sometimes. Your kid is just doing what they're supposed to do, which is to push the boundaries. Your responsibility as a parent is to keep your cool and establish firm guidelines while still holding your kid responsible when they disobey.

A Guide To Emotion Management

Everytime we set a boundary which isn't in tune with what our children want, there will be discord. They will comply on occasion, but most times, their curious natures will prompt them to act out or at least ask why they're being told to do something they don't want to. It's a natural reaction— if someone tells us to down a tablespoon of Benadryl and it's the last thing we want to do, we'd only do it *if we know it's good for us*. We're adults, so we have a grasp on what must be done for the sake of health and wellness. A three-year-old isn't quite there yet.

Many of our reactions— when it comes to our children— are adapted from our childhoods. For a moment, picture yourself back in your child-self, witnessing all the times you were penalized for having desires, wants, and emotions and not knowing how to handle them. Remember how you felt when you were reprimanded for making an innocent mistake. It could be that your tears or tempers were countered with "you're fine," or "don't be such a baby," or "just stop crying, it's not that big." Maybe you were shamed for acting in a manner that was inconvenient for the grown-ups around you. Perhaps you were spanked or told off for wanting a toy or a bowl of cereal at night and having a meltdown when your request was denied. Or, you heard the words, "you hurt me," and "you're making me mad" multiple times.

As a result, these are the feelings you may have internalized as a child:

- Everything I want is immaterial and should not be listened to.
- My feelings are wrong, and I should never express them.
- I should act as I am told to.
- My caregivers' feelings are my burden, and if I don't have a good image, they're going to be sad and it will be my fault.

You see the problem here? As you grow up, you begin questioning your inability to say no to atrocious demands, you over-think and feel bad about the world's opinions, and are constantly plagued by the need to be perfect. The body tends to remember what the mind may forget. It stores information from your past and tells you to repeat childhood patterns because that's what feels safe. The saving grace is that, while your brain is being wired during your childhood, *the wiring can be changed.* Yes, it will take time and effort— but it is worth it, especially when you are considering something as significant as ending a toxic inheritance of generational trauma. The very first thing you must do is learn the truth about feelings.

No one else can hurt you unless you let them, so stop saying things like "you hurt me" to your children. You are in charge of how you feel because your emotions belong to *you.* They are vibrations living inside of you. What you think and feel is more connected to your history and experiences, and how your life's story influences and draws from the present moment. In this sense, we don't create our children's moods; rather, we trigger them by the meaning we attach to the actions of others or the events around us. In addition, we may use our triggers as an opportunity to expand our knowledge and develop as individuals.

Everyone is allowed to feel what they do, including you and your children. If the adults in your life always treated you as if their feelings were more important than your needs, know that they were in the wrong. Their intentions may have been good, but they made an unconscious error that you can avoid. Feelings aren't the flu, and you shouldn't let your negative emotions get escalated whenever your child feels something that goes against the grain of your nature. We each have the right to establish whatever limits make us feel safest, while other people have the same right to experience whatever sentiments are prompted in them. You can teach your children the way to healthily express these sentiments, but you cannot, and should not, stop them from arising.

Learn to differentiate between empathy and codependency. Empathy allows you to put yourself in the shoes of your children to understand what they are going through. But, it also gives you the right to set boundaries. It's like knowing your children are allowed to have their feelings, and while you care deeply about them and are there for them, *your feelings do not need to be the same as theirs.* On the other hand, codependency is parasitic and can result in one of two situations:

- Your children's feelings must be in tune with yours, so they will have no needs, wants and desires of their own.
- Your feelings should be the very same as your children's, so you cannot have any separate desires

or an individual identity. You are what they have made you.

Naturally, your role here is to learn and show your children the way forward through empathy. The inner child who blamed themselves for their caregivers' distress is yearning for you to release them. You should tell them they can relax and take their fear away. I learned that I didn't have to change in size or shape to please anybody. Use the events of the present day as a trigger to remind yourself of whatever it was you needed to learn at the time. This helps rewire the circuit by surrounding our feelings of shame and self-blame with compassion. The tiny, apparently simple exercise of revisiting and loving the child within you will teach you the greatest truth about parenting.

Our role as parents doesn't need us to always be cheerful and unruffled. We provide a safe space for our children to express their emotions when we do the same, showing them how to recognize and own their own feelings of sadness and anger. In essence, we replace toxic ways of reacting to emotional turmoil, with healthy, nourishing ones. There's more where this comes from, and in the next chapter, we are going to go into the core of strengthening your parenting skills with responses that will enhance your relationship with your kids while allowing you to retain your individual identity.

Chapter 5

Developing New And Healthy Personal Habits And Traits

"When little people are overwhelmed by big emotions, it's our job to share our calm, not join their chaos."

– L.R. Knost.

At the onset, don't let the idea of "desirable" or "good" personal traits overwhelm you. When I speak of setting an example for our children, I don't mean that you need to be a lofty personality who is both revered and feared by those around you. The world has enough people who are loved for the sake of their apparent external portrayal of themselves. I, on the other hand, believe that the true test of mettle lies in knowing what makes someone worthy on the inside, within their tiny homes, surrounded by those who are closest to them. If the world loves you, but your own children skitter to their rooms whenever you set foot in the house, your qualities are nothing but superficial.

So, it is the simple things— compassion, love, understanding, devotion, and the ability to express yourself without hurting those who love you— that make all the difference. You could be the world's greatest politician or a steady, stable family man. It wouldn't matter. But when the final hour comes ticking, what will hold the most weight is how you are remembered by those who have loved you the most, those who have sought you out and looked at you as an example of someone balanced through all of life's tempestuous storms. Of course, it's great if people external to your family hold this opinion of you. But as they say, *charity begins at home.*

What Are Desirable Personal Traits?

When we look at personal traits in this book, our focus will be on characteristics that will make you a balanced parent. Remember, the mere act of giving birth doesn't make you a caregiver. It's what follows— the ways in which you show your children how much they are valued — that establishes your place in their lives as a mother or a father. In serialized fiction, there is a saying that goes, "Your audience needs to see. So, don't tell. *Show.*" Nowhere is this more pertinent than in learning to parent.

The first indispensable quality you must develop is resilience. It comes from a *true grit* mindset, which you express by showing your children that difficult situations and emotions are normal and more expected than they'd think. In the same breath, you also show them you can hang in there, feel what you are feeling and find a way through both the emotion and the situation with grace. It is your ability to recover from a setback without having a complete meltdown each time an issue rears its head. You don't let negative emotion fester inside or become completely swept away by it. You express the diffi-culty, the reason, and the aftermath *while working toward finding an answer.*

Next, there is the mystic sense of curiosity and wonder. Of course all of us will grow old. But we needn't lose the joys of our imagination and creative spirits in the process. The world is beautiful and terrifying, and yes, we will be afraid. But without the fascination that comes from exploring, discovering, and learning more about life, there is no sense or purpose to living itself. Children, in particular, are very adept at finding the wonders in the natural world. They are curious creatures who enjoy inflection and thought. Research itself says that just an hour of interacting with nature can improve your memory and attention span by 20% (Berman et al. 2012). So, grow up, but don't let your mind stagnate.

Coming in at third place is social intelligence. This demonstrates your ability to be a team-player. It's important in a family, because if you are constantly arguing with your spouse, your children will grow up with zero faith in rich emotions like love and compromise. Social intelligence will teach you to read deeper into your offspring's emotions and connect with them at deeper levels. Plus, social intelligence helps lead to the proliferation of another important trait, which is kindness.

Kindness is an important trait for many reasons. It helps you view the world from the lens of empathy. It makes you a person who thrives in multiple environments, because people *always* fall back on someone who cares. However, it is important to be kind, not because you are expecting a return or a favor, but simply because it is in your nature. Also, kindness does not need you to be a pushover. You have your own voice and boundaries in place, but you also recognize that other people will have theirs. In keeping your boundaries in place, you don't overstep and extend your limits to others, and if you must, you do so gently and with reasonable grounds.

Gratitude is one of the most important traits you can embody, because it will teach your children to appreciate what life blesses them with. Gratitude is the soul of a positive life outlook, and it will enrich your child's mind and nature. It will give them hope, energy, inspiration, and the ability to transform in response to changing circumstances. It must be cultivated, and the only way to do that is to model gratefulness in your own life. Choose gratitude as a fundamental tenet in your attitudes, and your children will be the better for it.

One of the most important traits you will learn and teach as a parent is self-control. This quality will enable you to regulate your impulses and feelings while recognizing the feelings of others. You will learn to manage your expressions, edit rather than delete them completely, and not be completely overrun by them. A key way to learn this is to delay short-term gratification for long-term rewards. As someone who is self-controlled, you can see the big picture and recognize the difference between short-term reactions and long-term implications. This will teach your children the golden rule of emotional management.

Finally, we have optimism. Positivity enables you to learn from difficult situations, and make the best of promising ones. A mere 3:1 positive to negative thought ratio will broaden your perspectives, make you aware of the larger social environment around you, and build creativity and receptivity (Fredrickson 2001).

How To Build New Habits Step By Step

In this hyperactive age of parenting, we fall back on assuming the best parents are superhumans who can multitask like they have ten hands and then some. In the process, we either think they're able to do it better because their life is easy or they have more willpower. Science disagrees. Parent A's notion that Parent B raised their kids happier because they worked from home or didn't have a job is false, because if they should be fixating on anything, it is Parent B's *discipline* and adherence to habit. You can work ten hours a day and come home to raise kids. It won't be the same as someone who works on raising them all their day, but this doesn't mean that they will raise happier children than you do. That's *entirely up to you*. So, before you go deeper into this section, begin with a deep breath and tell yourself, "I'm better than the petty comparisons."

The truth is, those of us who form healthy habits are able to overcome temptations like lazing on the couch as a reward for slogging it at work or just because we can. We can stay away from unhealthy takeout meals. We make the effort to consciously rise above procrastination. Our convictions also help us realize that life is deeper than the filtered half-truths that social media constantly tries to feed us. Research says that this is because we are on autopilot, and constructive action has simply become muscle memory, prompting us to eliminate harmful addictions from our day-to-day equations (Milkman 2021). Of course, you need to get to the stage where a thought moves forward to action, routine, and finally becomes a habit.

Begin by setting a definite mini-goal for yourself. Your manner of defining your mini-goal will help you form tiny habits that will lead to its achievement. So, don't go for some-thing really abstract like "read a story to my child regularly." You don't know the definition of regular, so this is you attaching a subjective element that will get in the way. Insead, choose something like "read to my child for half-an-hour every night." By making a bite-sized objective, you know what you have to do, which makes it easier for you to stick to the routine and visually see progress in your relationship with your kid (which, of course, is the bigger, ultimate goal).

Make a comprehensive plan. You're far more likely to progress toward each goal if you go a step ahead of just making it and also set aside a time-frame as well as where you'll do it and how you'll get there. A goal like, "I'll go walking with my baby every day is great," but what if you went into more detail? What if you made something like, "I'll return home after work, make dinner, and go for a walk with my child at eight p.m. for thirty minutes from Monday to Friday." Of course there will be variations depending on your work and circumstances, but having something concrete in place will comfort you and push you to achieve it, so the more detailed you can be, the better.

Enjoy the activities you do in the pursuit of your goal, and don't rush into bigger, more ambitious pursuits far too soon. We make the mistake of getting carried away after one day of doing something right. So, if I read to my child for half-an-hour on Monday, I may get exhilarated at her happiness and immediately decide to read to her for an hour on Tuesday. Then, when Tuesday night comes, I get overwhelmed because I don't have an hour to spend. Rather than that, I could have just focused on the designated thirty minutes and really enjoyed it with my daughter, just taking pleasure in the little ritual destined to bring us closer. That's what makes good habits special. They're there to comfort you.

Stay as flexible as you can. Fall back on some get-out-of-jail-free cards when work becomes too taxing or too demanding, and you simply cannot find the thirty minutes you need to read to your child. Instead, spend ten minutes before her bedtime just learning about what she's done during the day and reassure her that you're going to read a wonderful story the next day. Know that these set-backs are common and happen during the course of forming *every habit*. Some of us give up after one difficulty and never get back into things. But those of us who stay the course and return with our hearts and minds the next day are absolutely going to excel at transitioning a routine to a ritual. So, keep these emergency cards reserved, but don't let circumstances discourage you.

Finally, find good social support. We are always influenced by the behaviors of people around us, so if you want appreciation (which is natural) talk about your parenting highs and lows with your family and close friends. Don't make this a lone man's pursuit, because it is a joyful experience to be shared by everyone. You'll pick up useful information from them regarding what approaches are successful, and you'll create better connections which won't let you get away with slacking off. Good habits are actually contagious (Carrell, Fullerton, and West 2008), so there's a very real chance you'll be inspiring others along the way!

Becoming A More Attentive Person

It's so easy to overlook the things our children tell us sometimes. Since they love us and consider us to be their fortresses and shelters, they will tend to speak about little things that play in their minds— plus, they can move from thought to thought very quickly. It helps to learn attentiveness as a habit so you aren't caught unaware when they look at you with their innocent eyes and ask, "Did you listen to what I just said?" Here are some ways for you to be an emotionally attentive parent.

- Pay attention to the true nature of your child and reflect your understanding back to them. Observe what they like and dislike, what makes them mad, induces fear, and causes struggle. Based on what you learn, offer them advice and bolster their defenses so your child learns to see themselves the way you do— as an independent, self-sufficient young human being who has all the love they'll ever need to grow up and grow well. For instance, if they are struggling with their homework, help by saying,

"Goodness, these questions! It seems your homework is really difficult today, no? I know you can solve it all by yourself, so why don't we approach it (*and enlist the solution*)."

- Feel your child's emotional frequencies. You may not always agree with it, but when you show your children you can grasp what they are feeling, they bond with you. Vocalize their feelings and teach them verbal ways of expressing and arriving at constructive solutions. For example, if they are spending too much time alone, say something like, "You look sad being alone on this lovely day. Does it feel lonely?" When they express their emotion, teach them to find the solution. "Okay, I see you are sad. I get that. What do you think would help?"

- Share with your kid that you enjoy their company as well as your affection for them. It's crucial that your kid understands and accepts your affection for them. Hugs, laughing, and genuine expressions of delight in your child's unique character all go a long way toward transmitting this sentiment to your youngster. Having the intellectual knowledge that one is adored does not equate to experiencing that love.

- Respond with confidence and without any judgment. Don't tell your child how they should or shouldn't feel. Examine the cause of the emotion rather than the emotion itself. Teach your kid how to identify and regulate their feelings. Provide them with reasonable, age-appropriate guidelines. If your daughter intentionally takes her younger brother's toys, you may explain how difficult it is to share with someone so young. Have a conversation with her about the value of family unity, the dangers of hurtful behavior, and what she could do instead of snatching his things. If she acts the same way again, then move to making her take responsibility for her actions.

- Pay close attention to little details. Sharing more of life's little emotional events with your baby can help them immensely as they develop into an adult. Give your child an unexpected hug when you see that they are upset. Whenever you sense that they may be upset, ask them if they're all right. When you think your kid may benefit from it, spend some additional time with them. Talk to your kid about how they are feeling and engage in something special with them if they are going through a tough time, such as beginning a new school or a move.

Learning Self-Compassion

In simple words, self-compassion is having the grace to treat yourself with kindness when things don't go well. It is being aware of your feelings and learning to treat yourself with care, warmth, and understanding. In essence, it is you teaching your child that accountability and unforgiveness are not the same thing, and that while struggles and challenges are part of life, *everyone* goes through them and becomes stronger and better because of them. You, the parent or caregiver, might be brutal upon yourself at times.

It's easy to criticize yourself unfairly when you contrast yourself to other parents. When dealing with the stresses of parenting, practicing self-compassion may help you be easier on yourself. In addition, this is beneficial for both you and your kid. Self-compassion is beneficial to your emotional and psychological well-being. You'll be able to provide your kid more of what they need for healthy growth and development since your stress and anxiety will decrease. In addition, being a self-compassionate parent is an example your youngster may look up to. Encourage your child to understand that it's okay to make mistakes, to accept themselves, and to try again by modeling self-compassion.

Your child will learn to always have kindness for themselves as a consequence. Pause and notice your thoughts. Try to identify when you're being too hard on yourself. If, for instance, you label yourself as a "bad parent" after losing your temper with your child or being unable to teach them an important lesson, learn to distinguish between what is true, and what you are feeling in the moment. Also, ask if you would treat someone else you love this way, or if you'd help them find a constructive solution to the issue they are facing. If you'd do that for them, why not for yourself? Try your best, and learn as you go.

Self-Care As A Parent

Accounting for your overall, individual wellbeing will help you feel your best. When you're happy from the inside, you'll be encouraged to be the best caregiver you can be. Therefore, setting aside a few minutes for self-care, even if it's the last thing on your mind, is essential. There are many strategies available, and all of them are easy, simple, and won't take more than ten to forty minutes of your day. Consider it a social service of sorts, if you must. You're doing it to be the best, most wholesome version of yourself. I'm going to list some of my favorite ways here, but feel free to pick and mix, or experiment until you find your fit.

- Meditate, even if it's just for five minutes. If you're new to the world, you can even try guided meditation or yoga nidra. There's no dearth of applications, websites and online platforms to guide you along the way. I've found instrumental guided meditation videos on YouTube, so if the subject interests you, go on an online hunt. You can also experiment with different breathing exercises to reduce stress. A few cleansing breaths can work wonders for both the mind and body.

- Research has shown, time and again, that one of the best ways to unwind is to spend some time out in nature (Weir 2020). It can be immensely beneficial for your psychological well-being. A quick hike on a trail, a few minutes in a garden, or a brisk walk in the park — get creative and find a way to just connect with the earth around you. If there are absolutely no options, spend a little while watching a nature documentary instead of mindlessly scrolling through the lives of social media influencers. Landscape visuals via digitized mediums can be just as calming as being physically out in nature.

- Listen to music. It can be anything you like, so long as it helps you unwind. You don't even need to set aside a designated time to enjoy music. You can listen to it while engaging in other tasks like cleaning the house, feeding your child, or just getting work done. In the morning, try to listen to something upbeat when getting ready to own the day. It's a simple trick, but it goes a long way in raising your mood and enabling you to tackle whatever life may throw your way.

- Go for a walk. Exercise is a very real way to give yourself a serotonin boost, so if you don't have the time or energy to do jumping jacks or burpees, just a brisk walk for half-an-hour to forty minutes will suffice. The little extra activity will be sure to leave you energized for the rest of the day.

Besides these, there are many other self-care strategies you can incorporate into your life— you can join a book club or a nature lover's organization, read more books, try journaling or coloring for adults or even making mandalas. Eat well, get enough sleep (ideally seven to eight hours), and exercise regularly; these are the cornerstones of self-care that should never be ignored. Accept less than impeccable housekeeping, but always make time for the essentials, like doing the dishes, vacuuming, and washing the clothes.

The next step is to establish a consistent self-care practice. It's important to remember that it's precisely at those moments, when you feel most overwhelmed, that you need to take the time to focus on your own well-being. However, if, at any point in time, it feels that you are far too stressed, consider falling back on the expert opinion of a healthcare professional.

Building Resilience To Stress

Let's move one thing out of the way. Parenting and stress are pretty much bound to co-occur. You can't have one without the other. However, just because stress exists, it does not have to dominate over every aspect of your life or that of your family's well being. To achieve a sense of equanimity in the face of stress, you will need to bolster your mental health with a healthy dose of resilience. Mastering resilience will not only make you a more balanced, flexible individual, it will also help you set an ideal example for your children.

- Make your connections meaningful. The support, advice, and acceptance you need during good and terrible times may come through the solid, positive relationships you have with your family and friends. Participating in volunteer work or becoming a member of a religious or spiritual group are also excellent ways to establish additional significant relationships.
- While preparing for different outcomes, never lose sight of hope. Even if you can't alter the past, you can always plan for a better tomorrow. Being open to and anticipating change might help you cope with unfamiliar circumstances and take on hurdles with more conviction.
- In small ways, seek to make each day matter. Even if it is just waking up, working out for fifteen minutes, and really enjoying the first sip of a cup of coffee or whatever gets you going. Doing all these tiny things with intention will help you enjoy them.
- Don't shy away from the learnings of your past experiences. Recall times when you had to overcome adversity. Think back on the abilities and methods that got you through challenging circumstances. You might even use a diary or a blogging platform to reflect on previous events and draw conclusions about your present and future actions.

Friendliness Is A Virtue

The world is in dire need of compassion, now more than ever. Friendly people are a rare breed, and the mere desire to be one is laudable. Something as simple as having a warm smile can go a long way in making you approachable. A simple act of smiling, according to research, may trigger the production of endorphins, the body's natural feel-good chemicals (Riggio 2012). This means that even flashing a grin might boost your mood. When it occurs, sociability will come more easily. Of course, you don't need to smile when life is having it out with you. But during those positive moments, this little expression of warmth can show people you are approachable and you believe in sharing your joys.

Other than this, always be mindful of your body language when you approach others. People are naturally wary of someone who keeps their arms crossed all the time, or wears a frown perennially on their faces. These are signs that you're closed off and don't like interacting, which doesn't help your social image. Don't be afraid to approach others first— but be mindful of the social circumstances shaping your interaction. When someone is sharing a part of their life— even something as simple as how difficult their day has been— listen before you answer. Sometimes, the best people can do for others is listen without judgment.

Make the small details count. When you work somewhere, or if you're going to a parents' gathering, make the effort to learn other people's names, their childrens' names, what they do, and so on. These tiny things can go a long way in making you appear approachable. When you introduce yourself to someone, keep your posture easy and let them be at the center of attention. And of course, just use social gatherings as a way to let loose and have fun— you've earned it!

. . .

Becoming More Optimistic And Positive

Life is far more uncomplicated when the glass is half-full. Optimists enjoy better health and live more wholesome lifestyles (Lee et al. 2019) This isn't hard to believe, given that a) research has established it , and b) it's much more difficult to be happy in a mind that's always worried. Optimists are also more likely to persist toward their goals, experience more emotional health, and have lower reactivity to stress. In other words, you will make a happier parent if you embrace optimism as a way of life. Optimism is understood in how you visualize and define life's many events. To begin with, try to visualize life in the following ways:

- Your life is better because of the good things that you have done to make it so.
- Every positive sign points to better things that will happen in future.
- Positive events in one area of your life are signals that you will experience bounty in other areas as well.

Appreciating Your Own Progress And Efforts

Parenthood isn't a sprint, it's a marathon. It takes grit, determination, compassion, love, and the ability to overlook the inevitable small errors that will happen along the way (after addressing them, of course). While you enjoy and learn in the process, don't forget to be proud of yourself. You're here, and you're doing your best. That, in itself, is worth more than you'd immediately realize. Don't forget to stop in-between for a few minutes to just take a few deep breaths and say, "Look how far I've come. It only gets better from here on. I'm doing my best."

Consider keeping a "done" list somewhere you can see it—we have wonderful little magnetic lists available these days that you can pin to your fridge. Get one of these and write down all the tasks you want to achieve in a day's time. Whenever you complete a task, tick it off the list. This visual alone will give you so much satisfaction! It's also a great way to teach your kids the subtle art of time-management. Once each week, write down everything about parenting that really struck a cord with you and that you felt good about. Call the journal something wholesome like "The Monthly Wins." Remember, even something as simple as your child smiling at you and saying they love you is a big, big win. The biggest one in my book.

When it comes to winning at parenting, one of the things many of us fail to resonate with is discipline. In our minds, it often becomes the same thing as "punishment" although the two are as different as chalk and cheese. In the next chapter, we will learn more about positive discipline and how you can reinforce it as a way to enhance your relationship with your children.

Chapter 6

Positive Discipline Versus Punishment

"Don't worry that children never listen to you. Worry that they are always watching you."

Robert Fulghum.

P arents often get trapped between enjoying the time they spend with their children, and the need to discipline them. Raising tiny human beings into competent adults can be one of the most nurturing and fulfilling things we accomplish in our lifetimes. We experience a wide range of emotions that are both fulfilling and intense. When it happens, it can feel like time is at a standstill. Yet, when they are all grown-up and we look back on their childhoods, it always feels as if the time went by far too soon.

So, how do we ensure that, in the time that is given to us, we are able to teach them the secrets of a balanced, rich, and nuanced life? We want to be the best friends our children can ever have— but parenting goes above and beyond the tenets of friendship. A parent is *always* a friend, but a friend may not necessarily be a parent. How do we achieve that perfect healthy medium, where they turn to us both for advice, and also understand why we must guide them away from harm with a stern and gentle hand if necessary? Discipline isn't remotely concerned with you picking a fight with your children.

Rather, discipline's principle tenet is teaching our children to control and express their behaviors in socially appropriate ways. It is enabling our children to grow up into individuals who will be loved, and not shunned by the world around them. The concept can be confusing, and in the process, we may not understand that being harsh with children and disciplining them don't belong on the same page. As parents, we have a duty to teach our babies acceptable patterns of behavior that are essential for coexisting with others, and for being good people. There is no one-size-fits-all handbook on this— but just a bit of guidance should be enough to get you started.

Discipline Versus Punishment (Or, Positive Versus Negative)

Parents often make the basic error of confusing discipline and punishment and thinking that they mean the same thing. The differences, while subtle, are very significant. Both will teach children to adhere to rules— but one of them derives its sole existence from instilling fear, and only one teaches children how they can correct their behavior, so they become equipped with the right tools and understanding needed to evaluate situations and circumstances and act appropriately. Consider the following scenario: Marie and Joshua are having it out with each other over crayons. Marie pushes Joshua and they both start shouting at each other.

Their mother, sick of the children screaming in her house all day, raises her voice. "Just stop it, both of you! I'm so tired of this! You're not allowed to go out all afternoon because you've been so bad!" This is punishment. It will be effective enough in stopping the argument, but it won't cull the resentment between the children. As a matter of fact, they will find a way to keep fighting when the mother isn't around. The purpose of the punishment gets ruined in the process. She wants them to see that it's fighting that's bad, but instead, she ends up showing them they can do whatever they like, so long as they're not doing it in front of her.

On the other hand, imagine her mother says this— "Hand over the crayons to me. Neither of you will use them right now. Marie, just take a deep breath and tell Joshua why you are upset." She waits for Marie to talk, and also tells Joshua he will get a chance to voice his feelings. Next, Joshua lists out his reasons for his anger. The mother asks them to find a solution and present it to her before she returns the crayons to them. *This is discipline,* via which the mother has taught her children to think before they fight with each other, and come up with solutions that won't lead them to scream the house down whenever a disagreement flares up between them.

Discipline has two forms, positive and negative. Positive discipline is what teaches your children to cope with difficult situations and rise as capable individuals. *Negative discipline is the same as punishment, and we make the mistake of thinking that it is all that discipline is.* Negative discipline instills fear and involves harsh methods that are often punitive and counterproductive, and should be avoided as best as possible.

While no parent intends for their child to be physically harmed, tempers flare and things spiral out of hand even when the parents are doing their best. In the United States, the American Academy of Pediatrics is firmly against the use of corporal discipline with children. And honestly, I believe our children deserve better. The emotional well-being of children may be negatively impacted by negative forms of discipline such as spanking, striking, sarcasm, verbal shaming, or demeaning comments, which can teach children to resort to similar forms of punishment on other children or teach them to lie to escape punishment.

Uncovering Positive Discipline

First and foremost, discipline is not a synonym for punishment. The roots of the word can be traced back to Latin, where its literal meaning is *"to teach."* Life itself is the greatest teacher of all, and it is only when we fail to learn that situations become punishing. Discipline works best when it is fair and encouraging, rewarding good behavior and explaining the issues with bad behavior. Some parents mistakenly believe that discipline entails the use of physical force (such as beating or slapping the child) or excessively harsh words (such as screaming or threatening in the effort to instill obedience).

In no way does this qualify as discipline. When you discipline your child, you aren't trying to hurt or scare them into doing something. Rather, you are teaching them to behave responsibly and take pride in their ability to control themselves. The ultimate goal here is to help your children take ownership of their feelings and behavior through self-monitoring.

Using positive discipline will teach your children to adhere to a defined framework of expectations and routines. These expectations and routines contribute to the stability of one's social and private worlds. A child's early experiences at home may lay the groundwork for a lifetime of discipline. Eventually, this will have far-reaching consequences. Self-discipline entails doing things like going to bed and waking up at the same time every day, eating sensibly, working out consistently, and following one's interests in healthy ways.

Discipline in social situations involves adopting appropriate behavior in planned or impromptu get-togethers. Professional discipline, on the other hand, includes things like keeping on schedule, showing respect to superiors, keeping healthy interpersonal relationships, and so on. A civilization cannot function without discipline, and the importance of discipline in our society begins from the earliest stages of our educational systems— most of all, our roles as parents.

When a person grows up without any discipline in their lives, they become dull and directionless. They fail to understand why they must behave in accordance with established norms, and as a result they do whatever they like and then suffer the consequences. They are unable to handle crises and always end up in messy situations, needing others to bail them out as frequently as the sun sets.

For obvious reasons, we don't want our children to grow up and become utterly lawless. Good, positive discipline can help your child to grow into the best version of themselves and achieve success. Only through discipline can they incur the focus needed to win at life, respect those around them, be grateful, and understand the value of the time that is given to them.

Understanding Punishment And Its Negative Impact On Children

Have you ever felt like you are just at the end of your tether, your child has tested your patience beyond comprehension, and the only way forward is via a healthy dose of spanking? Whenever you resort to harsh measures to prove a point— including verbally shouting at your child, spanking them, or locking them up in their room until they behave, you could be contributing to a miscreant in the making, because your child isn't really learning *why* they're being treated this way.

They think the immediate issue is *you and your temper*. In their minds, they can continue with their misbehavior so long as they plan it out a little more carefully. The next time they lie or cheat or change their marks on the report card, they'll do it ever so slightly better, not because they're trying to make you love them, but because they think that this is a way for them to get away with what they've done, the only issue being your temper and finding a way to work around it.

The AAP (American Academy of Pediatrics) put forward a policy statement titled *Effective Discipline to Raise Healthy Children*. I'm going to recommend that each of you take a look at what healthy discipline stands for, according to the experts. The professionals emphasize the importance of focusing on teaching good behavior over the urge to punish using bad behavior (Sege et al. 2018).

Research has proven that forms of punishment like slapping, shouting or spanking don't work well when it comes to rectifying a child's behavior (S. J. Lee et al. 2013). This also applies when you shame a child for making a mistake that they don't understand— at their age, they must be taught to identify between right and wrong, because they're just trying to survive. Punishment is more than ineffective. It can also inflict serious damage on the child's long-term mental and physical health.

Spanking tends to increase aggression and anger in children. A study looked at children in twenty large U.S. metropolitans and discovered families employing physical punishment were caught in a toxic, negative cycle. The more they spanked their children, the more the latter misbehaved, which just prompted more beatings in response. Spanking also (and quite alarmingly) teaches children it's okay to cause someone pain when you're angry or frustrated, even if the person being hurt is someone they love. Later on in life, they become inclined to hit and hurt others when they don't get what they desire.

Physical punishments also raise the risks of injuries, particularly in young children who aren't eighteen months old yet. They may also leave measurable impacts on both the body and the brain (Durrant and Ensom 2012). Children who are spanked display markers of toxic stress and experience stunted cognitive development. A study found that spanking led children to have less gray matter— which is the core part of the brain involved with self-control, and also caused them to have poor performances in different IQ (intelligence quotient) tests (*Tomoda et al.* 2009).

The child's sense of self-worth is formed first and foremost by their parents' views of them. Spanking sends a kid the wrong message, even within the most affectionate households, particularly if the youngster is too young to comprehend why they are being hit. Parents invest a lot of energy into making their kid feel good about themselves. So the child does something bad, gets spanked for it, and concludes, "I must be bad."

The pain of being spanked can't be taken away, not even by a comforting embrace from an understanding parent. Even after the embrace is over, the youngster may continue to experience the effects of the impact. Later on, they may even model the "hug" as a way to get away with making a mistake-- which is actually heartbreaking.

We've talked about this before, but this is a good juncture to remember children love to imitate and model their elders. There is a classic story about a mother with two kids who would spank her daughter whenever the latter made an error. One day, to her horror, she came to her daughter's room to find her spanking the baby boy. When she asked her why she'd done that, the daughter's response was simple. *I'm just playing.* Hitting leads to its own perpetuation, so if you don't want your children to grow up believing that they can get away with

89

causing others physical and emotional pain, don't teach them to use it.

Spanking shows that it's alright for people to hit other people, and particularly that it's fine for elders to hit tiny people and stronger ones to inflict physical pain on more vulnerable ones. Children begin thinking that anytime there is a problem, it can be solved with a good old-fashioned swat. They will inevitably carry this model of interaction into future relationships with their peers and siblings— including partners and offspring.

In the moment, you may think a little spanking is harmless, and that you don't even do it "that hard." Most of the time, you're very gentle and loving. An occasional reprimand is help-ful. However, we humans have a tendency to remember the bad over the good. So, it's not surprising that children will hold onto negative messages far longer than nurturing ones. You may hit them only once in a blue moon, but *they will remember, especially if you acted out of anger and impulsivity.*

The message sent by corporal punishment is that violence is an acceptable way to express one's emotions or resolve conflicts. This is why the tone of the parent's voice during the spanking is just as memorable as the smack itself. You'll often hear that you're not supposed to teach your children anything when you're angry. If this were reinforced, spanking and verbal abuse would become obsolete. After the parent has cooled down, they may think of a more effective way to reprimand the child.

Shouting at young children and inflicting damage with words, even for a parent who is warm and loving, can cause mental health problems in children. Harsh verbal discipline is one of the fundamental causes of chronic depression and anxiety among young teens and adolescents, because in effect, they are constantly being told of the very many ways in which they are inadequate. Everyone who has ever been screamed at knows that raising your voice does not improve communication. Your kids are just like everyone else's. If you have to raise your voice to get their attention, they'll stop listening, making it more difficult to enforce rules and regulations.

Children who are screamed at tend to become more physically and verbally hostile. It's always an indication of frustration when someone yells at you, no matter the setting. Young ones are frightened and made to feel vulnerable by it. dTherefore, if shouting at kids is bad, then yelling accompanied with verbal diatribes and taunts is emotionally abusive (Gershoff et al. 2010). Anxiety, poor self-esteem, and aggressive behavior are only some of the long-term consequences. Children's perceptions of appropriate limits and their own worth are distorted as a result, making them more vulnerable to become bullies or get bullied.

Knowing When To Discipline

The inevitable question is— what age is appropriate for you to begin disciplining your child? The hardest part of beginning this lifelong dance is figuring out the happy medium to balance your toddler. The maddening truth at the heart of our need to have "perfectly" adorable babies doesn't help, because it points to a singular reasoning— in this developmental phase, it is the parents and not the babies who need to be disciplined. Without imbuing agency in your own life, there is no way you will be able to reign down the chaos that parenting a toddler will inevitably lead to.

Toddlers explore their world by making a mess of everything. It's just how they are. It can be frustrating to watch your baby litter the floor with food and toys, but discipling a two-year-old who is on the verge of an important discovery won't lead to anything constructive, and will likely result in complete failure. Therefore, before you discipline, make sure your expectations fit your family's circumstances. The very real truth is you can't discipline a child until they are two, which is the ideal time to prepare them for potty training.

If you go too hard too soon, you can increase your own frustration, which will definitely result in a battle of words and lead to a situation where you think parenting wasn't a great choice for you. Be kind to yourself and don't walk down that road. In 2013, a study highlighted that yelling at children daily was dangerous— as bad as hitting or spanking them (Wang and Kenny 2014). Inadvertently, you could cause long-term aggression, cognitive issues, and antisocial tendencies to take root.

There's no need to feel guilty if your child isn't ready for discipline just yet. The goal of discipline is to teach behavior, or to create consequences for misbehavior so that it is less likely to occur again. Your kid may feel like you're yelling into the abyss if they haven't developed the cognitive ability to connect the dots between an action and its resulting consequence. Consequences should be introduced around the age of 2. If a child isn't growing as a result of their parents' actions, then it's not discipline. And if your kid is not emotionally and cognitively mature enough, you are wasting your breath and may be doing permanent harm if you scold and reprimand excessively. Everyone will have a miserable time and nobody will learn anything. You shouldn't see this as giving up your responsibility as a parent in an effort to reduce disruptive behavior. It's like reserving your energy for when the stakes are higher. Here are some pointers to carry forward:

- Wait till your toddler is ready for potty-training before beginning to discipline them.

- Distract a child who is younger than two when they are acting out, rather than doing anything punitive.
- Avoid harsh verbal interjections at all times. This includes using insults, swearing and shouting.
- Finally, remember disciplining is not the intent to punish children for the sake of it; rather, it is to stop harmful behaviors from occurring frequently. Give them the opportunity to grow from their errors.

The Types Of Discipline

As time progresses, so will our access to divergent information sources. Today, there is no dearth of new literature on strategies to discipline our children. The novel ideas, however, are essentially all subtypes of three core concepts of effective discipline — positive, gentle, and boundary-based. Regardless of what you model, a kind and firm authoritative approach that employs consistent limits and teaches the value of consequences, while also validating the child's feelings, is the best way to go.

Determining the kind of discipline that is right for your family will, all in all, be a personal choice depending on your temperament, your child's predispositions, and the cultural and familial boundaries within which you operate. There is no single 'ideal' approach, but my only recommendation would be to always forgo punishment. You can very well take an eclectic approach combining a few techniques from each subtype of discipline, barring negative discipline, which I won't cover anymore.

The first subtype is positive discipline. It derives from praising and encouraging your child instead of focusing on punishment. It relies heavily on communication— parents literally explain everything to their children. They teach them to solve problems and work closely to develop constructive solutions. Positive discipline is often embodied in family meetings (interventions) and gentle authoritarianism to address behavior issues. To illustrate, let's take a hypothetical scenario of a seven-year-old refusing to do their homework. To employ positive discipline, a parent will sit down with the child and say something along the lines of, "I understand your teacher wants this assignment tomorrow, and you don't feel up for it. So, what can we do to get the work done so you can show your teacher you've excelled at what she asked for?"

Next is gentle discipline, which believes prevention is better than cure. Redirection is one of the fundamental tools used in this subtype, where parents typically steer children away from bad behavior. In gentle discipline, parents don't move within a mile of instilling shame. Instead, they employ tools like distraction and humor, the key being to help parents manage their own emotions while addressing the child's issues. Let's take the example from above, where the child is refusing to do their homework. With gentle discipline, a parent could respond by saying, "Would you rather write five hundred words on why you didn't want to finish your homework tonight?" Once the situation gets diffused with humor, the parent would look at the homework with the child and discuss ways to get it done as efficiently as possible.

Then we have boundary-based discipline, which focuses on setting limits with clear rules right at the onset. Children get choices and consequences for acting in certain ways. Children need limits in many areas of life, not only in terms of punishment. Children learn that respecting the rights of others is necessary for receiving the same consideration. So, if the child is resisting homework, the parent using boundary-based discipline would set a limit with a defined consequence such as, "I'm going to take your story book for a bit, but as soon as you finish the homework, it's all yours!" It's possible that boundary-based discipline is one of the most often used methods of correction among parents. It's also understandable— we want our children to learn that there are limits to everything in life, both good and bad. The understanding should be organic, and this form of discipline is a wonderful tool to instill it at a young age.

By now, we have covered considerable ground, and at this stage, you must be excited to try out all the new techniques and tools we've uncovered. But, I would ask you to pause and do some introspection for a minute. Before you go forward and teach your children all the ways in which they can experience life while also being within their limits and respecting boundaries, you need to turn the teachings inward. As the saying goes, you can't pour from an empty cup. So in the next chapter, we will discuss certain skills and virtues that will go a long way in helping you parent with relative ease.

Chapter 7

The Skills To Master As A Parent

"Raise your words, not your voice. It is rain that grows flowers, not thunder."

Rumi.

I n a room full of people who are closest to you, how much time would it take for you to say, "I'm close to me too?" All of us look at kindness as an abstract external concept—something that is to be shared with the outer world as a mark of how we were brought up.

Have Before You Give

Time and again, we've been taught that virtues are only useful insofar as they help us rise in the eyes of others. Yet, what about self-worth, self compassion, and returning an iota of the kindness we show to others back to ourselves? We look for these qualities when interacting with others and model them for our children so they know how to treat people when they grow up, *but are we also teaching them to reflect those same qualities back to themselves?* The best lessons, and indeed, the only meaningful ones, are taught from self-experience. Unless we know what self-love looks like, our attempts to teach it will always be hollow.

For instance, the quality of kindness is said to bring many health benefits. When we carry out an act of kindness for someone else, the pleasure and reward centers in our brains light up and there's a burst of serotonin— sometimes called the *helper's high.* The feel good hormone brings an overall sense of calm and also stimulates positive vibrations all over the body. Even so, with all the discourse around being kind to others, we rarely talk about being kind to ourselves.

Just what is it about the word 'self' that feels so off-putting? Do we, perchance, think we don't deserve the same kind of respect we bequeath to others? And if that is the case, is that how we'd like our children to feel when they grow up under the shadow of watching us do everything for everyone else and absolutely zilch for ourselves?

Self-compassion is, in fact, a vital part of sound mental health. Psychologist Kristen Neff (2007) has spent years studying and investigating the advantages of self-compassion, and she concludes that self-compassionate people are less likely to be self-critical, less nervous and depressed, and more satisfied with life overall. The idea is simple. A parent who cares about themselves will have concentrated efforts to be efficacious and put in a great deal of attention into how they raise their children. In other words, *you breed what you are.*

Evidence suggests that parents with low self-esteem will pass on the same sense of self-worthlessness to their children, because the latter learns to model the behaviors and actions of the former (Vinopal 2019). Researchers have discerned children can begin developing self-esteem from the minute they turn five. At this age, the brain works to build thought and behavior patterns, otherwise known as information packets or schemas that are stored in your neural networks over extended periods of time. Both experiences and feedback will lead to the fostering of positive thought patterns— *I am smart, capable and kind.* However, depending on the experiences the brain is exposed to and the feedback reflected back, negative schemas form as well— and these are much harder to rectify over time.

The brains of young children are particularly permeable, in that they are receptive to large amounts of information from the world surrounding them. Their neutral networks are only just beginning to take shape, which means that their schemas (while flexible) are very delicate and prone to be impressionable. They need to be exposed to the right kind of messages, failing which they can develop lasting issues with the ways in which they perceive themselves. Building self-esteem is more impactful that just praising our children. It's about giving children the right kind of praise.

As parents, we want to do more than exhort our children to do things correctly or well. We also want to laud them each time they try to achieve something, *even if they fail.* Every attempt is important— and while you could worry that too much bolstering of esteem would point to raising narcissistic children— the truth is different. Narcissists are actually inflicted with major insecurity issues and have zero self-esteem, which is why they keep needing others to show them how good and indispensable they are. You aren't working on raising socially inept children. Rather, showing them the value of self-esteem (by modeling it back to yourself) teaches your kids to be resilient and strong in their many dealings with life. You're working to praise their efforts, *not the outcomes.* This will give them the agency to face multifaceted issues later in life.

The issue with this method is obvious. Unconditional positive feedback, irrespective of the outcomes, is important— even crucial— but since so many of us were never raised on this healthy diet as children, it becomes difficult to project what we've never experienced. Our schemas are also much more developed, which means that we're at an age where low self-esteem is harder to fix because we've been exposed to the wrong messages over and over again, for far too long. Children do pick up on this, and eventually, they run the risk of believing they may not be good enough either.

When you get on a flight, the cabin crew will always instruct you to put on your oxygen mask first in case of an emergency. This isn't because they're telling you to be selfish— only practical. You cannot help your children if you're floundering for breath. Once you have the mask on, you can quickly and efficiently work on keeping others safe. The principle applies in all areas of your life. You must have self-esteem before you can teach your kids to model it. It can be incredibly difficult, especially if you are exhausted or feel like you're always failing— but raising kids who feel good about who they are will leave you more rewarded than anything else. So, while difficult, the good news is, it isn't impossible.

Self-esteem is not a single, simple quality. It is a mix between different traits that will not only help you project the kind of parent you want to be, but it will also show your children the importance of feeling good about themselves and just enjoying the time they spend at home. No one likes to be around people who are constantly questioning themselves, because like happiness, insecurity can be incredibly infectious. It can sit on the soul and dampen the most cheerful spirits. And, what's more problematic, is that once it takes root, it can take a lifetime of unlearning to understand you are more than how you were parented as a child. Your children needn't have the same harrowing experiences. In building your repertoire, you need to focus on a few essential qualities. We will look at them one at a time:

Compassion

When you actively take steps to be gentle to yourself, the compassion that you extend to those around you also becomes far more genuine. Consider these statements— you could even ask your close friends and family— and look at whether they are true for you.

- I tend to criticize myself abundantly for all mistakes I make, whether big or small.
- When I look back on my life, I focus a lot more on the mistakes I've made rather than the successes I've accomplished.
- I can be very cruel to myself and always feel it's my fault when I am struggling.
- When it comes to my goals, I push myself to the point of exhaustion.
- I have very high standards, both for myself and others around me.

If you agreed with most of these lines, and those you asked for help also said they sound like things you'd feel or do, don't be alarmed. Many of us have been raised to believe that brutal self-criticism is healthy and necessary if we want to live a life of high standards. We may even end up believing that an inability to be hard on ourselves will make us complacent, lazy, and ambitionless. Self-empathy is a technique that might help us feel more compassionate and open to helping others. Self-criticism is normal, but commencing with kindness for others might be a worthwhile place to begin if you tend to be harsh on yourself. Giving to others is a great way to learn to embrace and forgive yourself.

Self-forgiveness and self-care lead to greater authenticity in our acts of kindness toward others. Self-empathy strengthens our sense of agency and self-assurance, and it creates opportunities for friendship and common cause. Inspiring people with our purpose and defining our shared objectives is made possible through this. One further way in which self-empathy aids in forgiving others is by allowing us to better understand our own feelings.

The ability to show compassion for others grows in tandem with the degree to which we are able to replace self-criticism with self-understanding. The practice of compassion does not include submitting to being dominated by others. Instead, we may take decisive action when required and keep our doors open to everyone who needs them, including ourselves. Through developing both self- and other-empathy, we may tap into our innate resilience and forge genuine bonds with others, irrespective of any cultural, biological or social divides.

Empathy

When you can share the emotional vibrations of another person and understand their motives, you have empathy. In other words, empathy is being able to think from another person's perspective. However, it goes beyond existing as a base emotional response. The multidimensional framework of empathy includes cognitive and affective responses. In itself, it enables you to walk a mile in someone else's shoes, feel what they feel, experience what they experience, and know how they are being affected by something that is happening. It also means that while you understand and help someone else, you don't surrender your individuality to them completely.

In parenting, empathy allows you to cognitively grasp and tolerate why your children act as they do, and to not take it personally when they say hurtful statements in the throes of a tantrum— like "I hate you," or "I wish I'd never been born!" When you develop emotional empathy, you know that your children's vocalizations aren't targeted at you *personally*. Rather, they're the outcome of the situation which they're in, and which they don't like. A parent who is emotionally attuned to their child will have a secure attachment with them, which is critical for the child's psychological and cognitive health. A secure parent-child relationship lays the groundwork for:

- Children developing emotional sensitivity to the needs of others
- Overall emotional stability
- Learning to regulate emotions during childhood and later in adolescence, which in turn is a shield against grave issues like depression
- Better self-esteem
- Motivation to succeed
- Social likeability
- Anxiety regulation
- Less likelihood of social delinquency
- Lower risk of self-harm
- Reduced propensity toward aggression and violence
- Abstinence from harmful addictions

On the other hand, children growing up in low-empathy households are at greater risk of incurring:

- Self-esteem issues

- Constant mood spells, anger, aggression, and defiance
- Behavioral issues
- Anxiety
- Different phobias
- Addiction issues
- Social maladjustment and difficulty trusting others

Our approach to child-rearing and disciplining is shaped by empathy. Discipline that is too harsh or too punishing often leads to aggressiveness, hostility, and a lack of emotional regulation. As a result, the youngster may be much more vulnerable to the onset of emotional difficulties later in life. The sensitive parent, on the other hand, will know how to reprimand their kid without breaking their spirit. Consequently, developing empathy is essential— and to begin to be empathic toward your children, you must begin with empathy for the self.

Kindness

One of the most powerfully positive tools for building a happy and healthy home is kindness. Kindness helps you think for others, and while being thoughtful helps the recipient, it also improves your health and well-being. Practicing kindness alters the brain and brings lasting physical and mental health benefits. Our brains have mirror neurons that help us to learn by imitation— so when you model kindness, your children will learn it too. They'll learn to be good to the world at large and also to themselves. For young people to have an optimistic worldview, kindness is another important factor. As a consequence, they may be better able to concentrate and come up with original ideas in class, which would lead to higher grades.

It has been shown, says Adam Grant, an organizational

psychologist at the Wharton School of Business at the University of Pennsylvania, that middle school students who voluntarily help, cooperate, and share with their classmates have higher grade point averages and test scores than their less caring and less sharing peers. The beautiful thing about kindness is it activates the centers of your brain responsible for releasing endorphins. These are the body's natural feel-good hormones that give you a sense of pleasure. The more you indulge in little acts that inculcate generosity, the happier your overall state-of-mind becomes. Children who are treated with kindness are better equipped to cope with stressful situations and deal with the inevitable disappointments of life without taking their frustrations out on others around them.

Also, researchers have shown that doing something kind for someone raises their brain's serotonin levels, the chemical responsible for lifting their spirits (*The Science of Kindness* 2019). The release of serotonin has been linked to a reduction in sadness and the stress hormone cortisol in both the receiver and the donor of an act of kindness. Parents who are able to validate their children's emotions, regardless of whether or not they share those emotions, raise children who are more likely to approach others with kindness and empathy. Having this skill considerably improves the odds that a kid will grow up to be a socially competent adult who can appreciate the company of others and tolerate those who are different from themselves without resorting to hostility or conflict. When it comes to their kids, most parents want nothing more than to help them grow up to be compassionate adults. Similar to many other elements of parenting, the actions we do, rather than our words, will have a greater influence on our kids. So, rather than just instructing on the concept of kindness, it's more beneficial to demonstrate it.

. . .

Gentleness

A parenting style that evokes partnership between you and your child, gentle parenting relies on a willingness to get things done, rather than doing them due to external pressures. You, as a parent, become aware of the behavior you are modeling for your offspring. You encourage compassion, welcome emotional expression, and accept your child as an entirely capable, competent being. This doesn't mean there are no boundaries. Parents may be apprehensive when it comes to gentle parenting because they feel it entails losing control. We worry our children may fail to realize what is safe unless we take a harsher stance.

The good thing is, gentle parenting doesn't neglect boundaries or forgo discipline. In gentle parenting, you take a step back from reacting with anger or condescension, especially when it comes to justifying yourself. You don't say things like "I told you so," because your child is learning, and nothing good comes from you showing them you know better. You let your child know they have a partner in you, and you will keep them safe and help them learn. For instance, if you are a parent establishing expectations for a day of safe-playing in a park, you will tell them, "We are going to be safe by playing here, where you and I can see each other. Wave at me if you feel I am going too far back, and I will do the same for you."

Gentle parenting means always remembering a child is a child, and they cannot think or understand things the way you do. Their world is different from yours, and the thought patterns you have developed at your age will take them a while to get to. For instance, if your children are upset because they misplaced a toy or their day out in the park was cut short, ask yourself why they are reacting as they are. Their emotional maturity is still expanding— so when you acknowledge their reactions are likely quite appropriate for their stage of development, you also give them room to explore their reactions, thoughts and emotions while feeling safe, loved, and nurtured.

Respect

Mutual respect is the key to building healthy parent-child relationships. When you respect your children, you enable them to have healthier self-esteem. You also show them the reasons why respecting someone is so important, rather than just talking about doing it. Children learn by watching and feeling. Many parents believe that respecting children means we must give in to their demands— but it's not that. It's just knowing how to interact with them. For instance, you wouldn't scream at your partner or a friend in public, or expect your partner to leave whatever they are doing and come to talk to you.

In the same breath, if you order your children around, it will do much more harm than benefit to their well-being. They'll grow up feeling like pushovers, giving in to all demands no matter what the cost to their mental health may be. Always acknowledge their good efforts— no matter how big or small. Remember to use the golden words, please; thank you; and sorry often. If your children bring you something, always show how grateful you are. When you want them to do something for you, talk to them as you would talk to an adult whose help you are seeking.

Self-Care Skills

A parent is allowed, and as a matter of fact, deserves to have their own life, separate from their existence as a caregiver. Always remember to turn to your senses to understand what kind of care you need. Sometimes, a simple cup of hot tea can work wonders. On other occasions, you may need to call a loved one, read a book, book a morning at the spa, or devote more time to introspection. Whatever it is, your sense of sight, touch, sound, taste, and smell will guide you. Take joy in the little things. Marvel at how green the plants around you look, take a warm nap, listen to a funny podcast about parenting, indulge in your favorite dish once in a while, and turn to natural ways of comfort like lighting an incense or burning a fragrant eco-friendly candle.

Self-care does not mean you are separating yourself and doing something selfish. It means you are taking care of your mind and body so you can take better care of others. Parent-hood is not martyrdom, which is a mistaken equation far too many of us make. Plus, it can be the simplest thing— all you may need to feel upbeat could be a nice song and allowing yourself to sing or dance with abandon. Don't feel guilty for loving yourself, because that's not what you'd want your children to feel, right? How would it seem if they grow up thinking, "I'm not going to do anything for myself because it's selfish and I don't deserve it?" If you don't want that life for them, don't emulate it now.

At times, self-care will also need you to be strict with yourself. If the news feels too corrupt, or the lives of influencers online gives you a headache, take a conscious break from social media. Don't get caught up in a web of expectations, because the world you're seeing is all smoke and mirrors. You don't know how these people are really living their lives, all you can do is make the best of your own. Remember, you've got this, and you get to have fun in your own ways within your resources. Take a few deep breaths, and practice positive self-talk from time-to-time. Keep room for a minimum of one self-care activity each day.

Be upfront with your family and let them know when

you're taking a time-out, and tell them it's healthy— as a matter of fact, *let your children know they should do this on a periodic basis as well.* Self-care also brings with it the opportunity to make precious memories with your family. Take your children out to get ice-cream on some days, get them to participate in yoga or meditation with you, garden together, or read a page from your favorite book each day. As you show your children the value of turning inward, they will learn to soothe and care for themselves in times of stress. Ultimately, this will allow them to grow into healthy individuals who invest in healthy families of their own, building up to a communal collective that believes charity begins at home.

Naturally, when we think of doing so much with our children, we realize the value of building solid connections with them. We will look at this in greater detail in the next chapter.

Chapter 8

Building Positive Connections

"All things are connected like the blood that unites us. We do not weave the web of life, we are merely a strand in it. Whatever we do to the web, we do to ourselves."

Chief Seattle.

I've always been an involved parent. It's something I take pride in, but it also gives me joy and sustenance. One of my favorite things to do when my children were young was to read to them on a daily basis, at bedtime. Another thing was just talking to them, taking their opinions on things, and letting myself be awed by their dry wisdom— sometimes more profound than that of an adult. Later on, I came across a piece of research done by child psychologists Betty Hart and Todd Risely. In 1995, they studied language development and how home experiences affected young children. They began the study with a group of same-aged children, and went on to find that the extent to which their parents communicated with them mattered immensely (Hart and Risley 1995).

Healthier communication (both frequency and word quality) influenced their children's vocabulary development. It also resulted in better IQ (intelligence quotient) and literacy skills— all conducive to eventual success. Likewise, I also found that by eighteen months of age, the vocabulary your child develops can be highly predictive of their future academic prowess. As parents, therefore, we have a duty to connect with our children. This doesn't mean I'm asking you to read Tolstoy to them when they're two— although if that's your cup of tea, go for it. Even simple things like talking gibberish (the language all children love), cooing, using love and appreciation in your words, singing, or chattering with them can go a long, long way. Other instrumentally helpful means include pointing to pictures between 12-24 months of age and helping them form associations; and reciting phrases from books when they are between 3-4 years old.

When it comes to connecting with our children, the key phrase remains constant— *the earlier, the better.* After the horrors the world faced between 2020 and 2021, there has been an increased focus on educating our children at an early age, and from the limits of the home. Today, more than ever, we are focused on child care programs, home visitation programs, and calls-to-action that will help us build real, effective relationships with our offspring. When they are born, babies have over a hundred billion nerve cells that make up the sum total of their cognitive matter. These nerve cells connect and communicate with each other, resulting in the circuits that help us learn, think, and succeed. What's remarkable is that these neurons move at a remarkable rate of seven hundred connections every second during the *first five years of life.* So, no points for guessing that the most fundamental phase of a child's social and cognitive development is between the ages of 1 and 5. Peak development of many important pathways of the brain will happen during the very first year of a child's life. This includes their sensory pathways like vision and hearing, and their language pathways.

The rate and timings influencing brain development have a lot to do with genetics, but the strength and efficacy of the circuits influencing these developments have a lot to do with our interpersonal relationships and social interactions. Dr. Shonkoff, the Director of the *Center on the Developing Child*, deems that *serve-and-return* interactions occurring between children and parents play one of the most important experiential roles shaping the development of the young brain. So, what is the basis of this serve-and-return interaction? All of your everyday conversations— the back-and-forth that happens between you and your child, make this interaction what it is. It includes even the little things that are seemingly so silly, like cooing, chatting, singing, and other verbal forms of adoration. Research also reveals that there is a very strong relationship between a child and a responsive, loving adult. This relationship can act as a protective barrier against the detrimental effects of stress on a developing brain.

Connection Over Correction

In their youth, children will have a ways to go before they can grasp the power of emotions and adapt different, appropriate ways of expressing them. Connection before correction is a mode of positive discipline that allows you, as the parent, to connect with your child's state of mind, experience, feeling, need or want, before you teach or try to correct their behavior or mode of emotional expression. For instance, let's say your child is playing with legos on the living room floor. After a while, they get bored and get up to leave. All the legos are still strewn about the floor. In your haste to teach them to clean up after themselves, you may say something like, "Clean up or there won't be any legos to play with tomorrow!" This is you appealing to a negative emotion like fear and using it to get your child to do something. In the long run, it could become very counterproductive because your children will associate everything that's "negative" with *you*. Connection before correction would mean you respond to your child's behavior with something like, "Hey, did something else catch your attention? It's okay to move on and play with another toy! But before you do that, you'll need to clean up so you have room to play."

Some situations may arise where you'll find their emotions aren't quite on par with yours. Their anger may feel too intense in the context of a specific circumstance— and you'll be exasperated, wondering why they're so upset about the shape of a pasta or the color of the sky. In these cases, you can always offer a hug. Embraces embody connective experiences that'll help your kids tone down their emotional outbursts. After they calm down, you can reason with them, and show them that regardless of the shape or color, pasta is delicious and the sky is beautiful.

Crushing Barriers To Connection

As humans, we are always alternating between the need to protect our children and a higher desire to let them learn on their own. We want to be their friends, while also keeping parental boundaries in place. We wish for them to not face any hardships, but paradoxically, we also know that without hardships, they won't learn or grow. We hurt when they go wrong, but we understand that mistakes are the only route to sustainable learning. These paradoxical behaviors come forth to result in the barriers hampering our communication channels with our children. This doesn't mean these thoughts or paradoxes are unnatural— they're as innate as it gets. However, it's how we express our ruminations that causes conflict, both for ourselves and our children.

Offering Understanding And Safety

To address issues that may arise, you need to look at your child as an individual being who deserves to be respected. Rather than thinking that trust comes naturally because you're their parent, consider what it would be to earn the trust of someone outside your immediate circle. It would take time and effort from your end. It's no different for your child. Once they see they can look up to and lean back on you as a source of understanding, love, and safety, they'll instinctively know you won't lead them astray. They'll also realize that if you steer them away from one specific direction, there is a good reason for it. In time, they will follow your advice because their reflex will tell them "This is right. They're saying this because they want something good for me."

The first thing that builds trust is listening without judgment. Recognize your child's words, and try to understand the underlying implications of each verbal message. If, for instance, your kid shouts, "I hate you Mom!" she isn't saying she hates you. She's mad at something you've made her do— so think of why this is relevant in the current context. You can show her you understand by reflecting what she is feeling. So, you can say, "Are you sad because the playdate ended? I know it can be difficult. But you know what? Let's go home now, and before you know it, there will be another playdate even nicer than this one!" This gives rise to a positive core belief— *my parent hears what I'm feeling. I can talk about it. I'm safe.*

Next, take the listening stage a step further and attune yourself to what your child is saying. Attuning allows you to anticipate your offspring's needs depending on different verbal and nonverbal cues. For instance, it helps you understand that a child who is throwing a tantrum may just be tired. It tells you to take the focus away from punishment and calm your child so that they come back to the plane of level thinking. They'll do this when they realize their needs are important and are being heard by you. Focus on their eyes and hold their gaze. Be gentle, and let them know what sincerity can do. Children will ask you for help— whether they do it verbally or nonverbally. The minute they find you are addressing their pleas, they will build trust and become more open with you.

Respond to emotional expressions with support and valida-tion. When a child speaks on something that points to them being afraid, always show you're willing to help them to stay and feel safe. So, say something like, "I know you feel fright-ened. Let's figure out a way to help you counter that." Validate them instead of being judgmental and saying something that'll hurt their feelings like, "Monsters don't exist, it's pointless being afraid of them." You don't want them to think their feel-ings are invalid or silly. Fright is a very real feeling, and if they don't learn to address it, it will come back to haunt them later on. Let them know they can come to you for help without getting invalidated.

Gaining Your Child's Trust

Avoid relying on white lies when it comes to communi-cating with your children. If you don't like something they are doing, don't get them to do something else with the help of a lie or a false promise. Instead, take a minute to yourself, and think of a way to help them come to a better response by themselves. This will also allow your children to match verbal and nonverbal routes of communication and reduce any blurred lines. It will teach them positive moral ethics and the values of being upfront about how they feel and what they stand for. Identify core boundaries and set them in place.

If you're wondering what effect this has on children's ability to trust you, the answer is, quite a bit. Trusting that events will unfold in a certain sequence helps children keep their senses intact and prevents unnecessary relapses into thinking they are in danger. An alternative kind of trust is fostered via the establishment and maintenance of limits, and that is the faith that a parent would protect one's well-being and honor one's values. While it's understandable that kids might be offended by a strict rule like "no smacking," they'll likely come to respect it as they become older and realize that you're protecting them from harm.

Always remember that it's okay to make mistakes. Show your children you're human, not a perfect rendition of an abstract concept that is above wrongdoing. They can't reach up to those standards because, well, to be human is to accept there will be flaws. Be open about your fears, shortcomings, struggles, the emotions they lead to, and how you work through them. This will teach them to accept their own shortcomings and find sustainable ways to enjoy life *with* them. In the same breath, also teach them the value of being careful with what they share outside their immediate circle. In all these cases, you are showing them the importance of boundaries— something that will keep them safe and help them grow for the rest of their lives.

Repairing Broken Relationships

All of us have those moments when we feel bad for being too harsh with our kids or doing something different from what we'd wanted to. I remember each time I was too hard on my children when they were having a meltdown. In retrospect, it's difficult, often impossible, to bring them to a calm headspace once they're in that zone. This is why so many of us react out of anger. Then, when the tides are low and we realize we've hurt them, there's instant regret. Many of us choose to let it slide because we think they're kids, they'll forget about it. The thing is, children do remember, and it is important to engage in relationship repair after we've been rougher than we'd intended.

It is essential to make an effort to restore the link with your child after a difficult parenting moment. This not only helps us develop our ties with our children, but it also teaches them compassion and avoids any trust gaps from expanding. Taking the time to speak about the things they regret doing is the first step in teaching our children to admit their mistakes and realize how their actions affect the people around them.

To begin, make an effort to calm down. You may try anything like eating, taking a shower, going for a walk, or even simply sitting quietly with your eyes closed for a few minutes to see if it helps you unwind. Give yourself permission to feel a variety of emotions, including hopelessness, rage, and fear. You deserve it. Some people need to vocalize, chant, or draw out their ideas, while others need physical movement. Find out what it is that puts you in a more balanced state of mind and make it a priority. The first step is the hardest, because when you're that angry or frustrated, the last thing you may want to do is calm down. Essentially, you need to reach a stage where you can step away from thinking, "Man, I hate this all," to think, "Okay, I reacted in anger. But what does my child need from me right now? What will make this a learning experience?"

Reach out to your child once you have taken a minute to calm down and regroup. A soft voice and a loving gaze are great ways to ease into a conversation. Invite your youngster to listen to you while remaining calm. You may try saying, "Hey, I made a mistake and would like to speak to you about it." If the door is closed, always knock on it before attempting to address them. Don't force anything. If you hear no response, walk away and come back an hour or half-an-hour later. Then, knock on the door once more and say something on the lines of, "May I please have a minute of your time? I promise it won't be too long." Once you're in, sit down beside your child, or sit nearby.

Ask how they felt about your shouting, or whatever it is that you wish you hadn't done. If your child is a toddler, try saying something like, "Hey, were you scared when I yelled?" Brace yourself for an emotional outburst— your child was likely overwhelmed and may shout, "YES!" or turn away completely. Give them enough time to express whatever is going on in their minds. If they are older, say something like, "I feel bad about my behavior. Are you mad at me? It's completely valid if you are. I'd like to hear your thoughts." Let them say whatever is going on in their minds and bodies. The more they express, the more they'll process what has happened. This will tone down the fire in their grudge.

Validate their feelings by giving a name to what you did wrong. So, if you shouted at them because you stepped on a lego, don't go to a place where you end up apologizing but also blame them for leaving the lego. You can teach them to not do that when the hurt is healed. For now, just tell them, "I feel bad I shouted so loudly at you. I shouldn't have done that." Once you have established a calm front for both of you, take time to tell them why you were angry. Don't yell, don't judge. Simply take them out and let them know leaving legos outside can be dangerous because people may not look where they are stepping. They'll learn to identify that something they did caused unintentional hurt, which will help them form associations.

Look your child in the eye and tell them you are sorry, from the bottom of your heart. Express your sorrow with hugs and be emotive. Reassure your youngster that you intend to change your behavior and share your plans to do so. Talk about what you're going to do next. Keep in mind the things you've spoken to your children. Put the instructions in writing where you can easily see them. The way you handle the next stressful situation will have a significant impact on your child's faith in you. Having your children trust you even when things don't go as planned may go a long way toward keeping your connection strong. Your child's faith and confidence in you will erode if you have more regrettable parenting moments. Your child can start to lose hope in you and doubt that you'll always be available to them, and that attitude might spread to other areas of life.

In the event of a frightening and traumatic interaction between a parent and child, such as physical or verbal abuse, substance abuse, threats of abandonment, or extended periods of separation, it may be impossible to recover without the assistance of a trained mental-health professional over the course of several years. Please think about seeking professional assistance if you've been through tough situations that have affected the way you relate to your children. Self-help literature, conversations with trustworthy friends, journaling, and professional medical and mental health care are all possible avenues for obtaining support.

By now, you must have realized that balance lies at the heart of all efforts to raise healthy, confident children. Parenting can feel like walking a tightrope, and you want to make sure you're not crossing or overstepping into any one domain far too much. Because, as the saying goes, too much of something can be a poison in itself. In the next chapter, we will discuss this concept in greater detail.

Chapter 9

Avoid Extreme Parenting, Overindulging And Overbearing Your Children

"Adults who are respectful of children are not just modeling a skill or behavior, they are meeting the emotional needs of those children, thereby helping to create the psychological conditions for children to treat others respectfully."

Alfie Kohn.

We've all been in situations where we've felt like we need to do something extra special to make it up to our children. In our haste to show them how much we love them, we end up buying expensive presents, giving in to their whims about eating out or consuming junk food on multiple days of the week, or allow them an added hour of screen time. We tell ourselves it's okay— a little pampering never does anyone harm. Unfortunately, these patterns tend to get entrenched over time. Both you and your children begin relying on them. Whenever something goes wrong, your child looks to you for these comforts, and in time, they also begin relying on them in the future. When they get hurt as teenagers or adults, they latch on to the harmful things that they associated with "comfort" as a child. They spend excessively in the attempt to reward themselves, they eat out all the time, and they mindlessly surf through social media. Too much of something is never good.

The Dangers Of Overindulging A Child

Have you ever been shopping with your kids and had to say "no" when they begged for a toy or sweets and then, they threw a tantrum until you caved in? Your children's cries would be temporarily silenced. However, this also guarantees that every trip to the store will be a struggle. Providing excessive rewards to youngsters too early and for too long might have negative effects. This is when an adult provides for a kid in order to satisfy his or her own desires, rather than those of the child. In other words, you are giving the child the toy because you want them to be quiet, not because they are crying for it.

A while back, one of my friends had their daughter go to college to get a degree in information science. He was a very excited parent— as we all are when our children begin taking flight. In his mind, he wanted the very best of outcomes, so he ended up sending his daughter's head professor an email every week, outlining all the areas in which his child was falling back or needed help. Of course, his intentions were from a good heart. But from a third person perspective, it is possible to see where he could have gone wrong. When the professor decided he'd had enough, he offered a gentle solution. He let my friend know his daughter was capable enough, and that he should trust and respect her individual decisions to approach and ask for help, or solve things on her own.

The above scenario also pointed to a kind of overindulgence. When you overindulge a child, you are giving them too much of a good thing, too soon, and for far too long. You allow them to have experiences that aren't appropriate for their interests, talents, capabilities and age. In essence, you are addressing a core anxiety that is bothering you over what your child needs to grow and develop. My friend acted as he did because *he* was anxious about his daughter's performance. The daughter herself was doing well enough, and confident that she would excel in the year end evaluations. Similarly, when you give a child something because you want them to stop crying, you're doing it because the sound of their crying is bothering you. You're not thinking of the long-term implications of rewarding their behavior, even if you know it isn't behavior you should reward. Here are some cases where overindulgence is apparent:

- You give too much. Providing too much of anything, whether it be toys, diversions, or technology, may have negative consequences. Children need rest, yet they should also learn to occupy themselves.
- You nurture too hard. Another aspect of overindulgence is when parents stop their children from developing independence. This might include things like doing your child's schoolwork on their behalf or protecting them from any negative feelings they may have, instead of showing them a route to healthy expression.
- You are not disciplining your children. Inadequate parenting, including the lack of discipline and proper boundaries, may hinder a child's development of self-control throughout adulthood. If your youngster is having a tantrum, for instance, you shouldn't give in every time, because they'll just

learn that the best way to get what they want from you is to have a meltdown.

Parents overindulge for many reasons, many of which are well-intentioned and loving. They want their kid to be happy, they may be financially secure and able to contribute more, or they may want to give their child opportunities they didn't have growing up. It's also possible that they're simply trying to make it through the day and that giving in to a fussy kid is the quickest and easiest way to do so. Overindulgent parents often lack even a fundamental knowledge of how their actions may affect their children's development. In the rush to make our children "happy" or fulfill all their expectations, we forget the one important rule of parenting-- we must raise our children to be capable, and we cannot do that if we continuously give in to their every fancy and whim.

If you are worried you may be overindulging your child, there are three questions you can ask yourself to get an idea.

First, can your actions harm the child's development in respect to their age and circumstances? For instance, if you are still bottle-feeding a four-year old child, you are likely allowing them to develop a habit that shouldn't exist at that age. The NHS (National Health Service) recommends that children should learn to wean from the bottle and drink from an open cup by the time they are a year old.

Second, are you providing things in excess of your family resources? When you are spending time, energy, money, or other expenditures on your children, it is important to consider if you are actually digging into nonexistent reserves and doing more than what you can afford. If you are sacrificing your own health, or not saving enough for your household while catering to your child's tantrums, there's a good chance you are overindulging them.

Third, ask yourself if you are giving your child what they want because you're doing it for them, or whether you just want something in return. If you are giving them an expensive video game or toy because you want them to stop throwing a tantrum, *your want* becomes the key player here. You're indulging them, not because you think the toy or the game is something that will really help them or make them spend time productively, but because you want them to stop screaming and hitting you.

Naturally, these patterns do not point toward emotionally mature children who can take responsibility for their thoughts, feelings and actions. There are a few reasons why.

- Overindulged children take no accountability. They always believe they'll get what they want regardless of what they do, so a time comes when the parents have little to no control over their children.
- Children learn that they are not required to adhere to regulations when there is no discipline in place. They might develop a false sense that the rules do not apply to them if they are not consistently enforced. They start to see themselves as exceptions to the norm and start to feel that they are better than everyone else.
- Individuals who have been overindulged as youngsters have a tendency to lack basic functional skills and do not aspire to grow personally or build meaningful connections as they become older.
- Overindulgence can contribute to dysfunctional thought patterns in adolescents.
- Children who face overindulgence are unable to delay gratification. If they want something, they

need to have it immediately— and that isn't how life works. When they grow up and find they can't cry or scream or whine away to get what they desire, they can either become depressed, or develop socially deviant behavior patterns.

- Your children begin associating happiness and love, which are very important emotions, with money and gifts. They learn to think that even if they can't be around company or show loyalty, they can win over anyone if they indulge or overspend on them.
- Children can't properly care for their possessions when they have an abundance of expensive technology, fashionable apparel, and playthings. In certain cases, an overindulged youngster just won't care if something is damaged or lost. Because of this, they won't develop a sense of responsibility.
- It has been scientifically shown that youngsters who are spoiled suffer from issues throughout adulthood. An overindulged youngster will grow up to be an adult who is chronically unhappy. A lot of them say they often overeat and waste money (Bredehoft 2021).

The Opposite Pole: Being An Overbearing Parent

We've established that overindulgent parenting can be messy. The polar opposite, however, is hardly any better. There are times when we cannot bear the thought of our children making mistakes. The idea of them being wrong about their homework or them not making helpful decisions when you're not around to help them, can be very hard to digest. So, some of us go an entirely different route from being pushovers and giving in to all our children's whims, and go on to act as control freaks instead. Overbearing parents generally demonstrate two kinds of parental control— behavioral and psychological.

Some degree of behavioral control is crucial for a child's healthy growth and development. Its purpose is to keep an eye out and make sure they're behaving properly by socially acceptable standards. Behavioral control of the overbearing kind refers to micromanaging your child's actions and supervising every particular activity they partake in. Overbearance in this category involves a parent disciplining a child's behavior to the point where they have no opportunity to learn from their mistakes, monitoring all their whereabouts, and running the remote control on their social lives. While regulation is important, so is autonomy.

Autonomy helps a child build their own identity with confidence and the reassurance that should they need any help or assistance, their parents will be there for them. Individuation — the development of the individual identity— is an essential component of transitioning from adolescence to adulthood. A parent who controls every aspect of a child's behavior will make it very difficult for them to develop this kind of an identity. Once again, the key lies in a happy medium, because children should not be allowed to run lawless. Parents need to give an adequate structure which they must adhere to, and within this structure, they should have their own individual freedoms.

For instance, if my child is nineteen and going out to a friend's home for the night, I set a structure which gives her four broad rules:

- Once she reaches her friend's home, she leaves me a message.
- She alerts me if she needs anything at all.
- I have her friend's number as a backup.

- She calls me in the morning and lets me know all is well.

Within this broad structure, she has her individual role to play, and enough room to grow, expand, and nourish her mind and identities. If I tell her she can't go or go all Black Mirror and spy on her, she'll learn to do the very things I'm trying to protect her from— and worse yet, she'll hide what she's doing from me.

The other form of overbearing parentage is manifested through psychological control. This refers to hindering the child's cognitive and emotional development. Parents who have experienced childhood trauma and cannot (or will not) recover from it, risk becoming unresponsive to their childrens' needs. They invalidate, constrain, and manipulate their childrens' experiences to get them to do what the parent wants over what the child needs. They also repeatedly stifle and shun the child's ability to express emotions independently. They may teach the children to develop a parasitic relationship where the child believes that the only source of happiness and validation in the world can come from the ones who refuse to give it— aka, their parents.

Through the parent-child connection, controlling parents affect their children's emotions, beliefs, and ideas through the use of guilt, love withdrawal, displaying disappointment, disapproval, and humiliation. They also want their children to be emotionally inseparable from them. For instance, if a mother repeatedly tells her son that he's not being a good child if he won't take care of her in her old age, she is (even with the best of intentions) psychologically manipulating him to associate a quality (goodness) with something that she deems as necessary for her own end. Children of parents who exert psychological control over them may grow up thinking their parents are overbearing and domineering in a variety of ways, including being overprotective, possessive, imposing, and inducing guilt.

Danger Zone: Breaking A Child's Spirit

Naturally, overbearing parenting will exhaust the children who are at the receiving end of it. As a parent who wants their child to succeed— no matter what the cost— a strict caregiver may insist on maintaining an iron-clad code of perfection that their children must adhere to. From piano to gym, karate to olympiads, they will do anything possible to give their children a head start at life. In doing so, as a journal found in 2011, they may fail to make their children healthier, happier, or even more successful. A stressed, exhausted child hardly has time to worry about uplifting qualities. They're too busy trying to keep up with their demanding parent's expectations to care about their own joys. So, it's possible that racing from one engagement to the next is depleting your child's energy and your wallet without providing any meaningful benefit.

You're fighting nature. When it's safe to do so, let your children experience the repercussions of their actions. To put it another way, you'll have to put up with your kid doing things you wouldn't do or making choices you disagree with. It's not easy to let go of the reins if you haven't done it before. I learned this the hard way, as did my daughter. When she was young, we were in the backseat of a cab. I kept holding on to her because I was afraid she'd tip and fall if the car hit an unexpected brake. She kept on resisting my attempts, scratching and screaming each time I reached out to hold her close. A time came when I realized this wouldn't work.

So, I calmed down and told her, "Hey, okay. I won't hold on to you. Just sit on my lap and hold the sides of my legs. Let's see where we go from here." Lo and behold, at the next swerve, I wasn't holding on to her and she almost toppled, but since she was on my lap, I reached out and grasped her immediately. She learned the meaning behind my persistence, and stayed quiet as I held her for the rest of the journey. Sometimes, children need to fall to learn— as do all of us. Your role is to make sure the fall is as gentle as possible, not stop them from learning altogether.

When you focus on controlling every aspect of their existence, you stop all creativity from developing. Consciously or unconsciously, you tell them, "There's only one correct way for you to do this, and that is the way I'm telling you right now." You stop them from looking for different solutions or engaging their own thoughts, logical brain, and creative mindset to solve issues. Later in life, this kind of one-directional thinking will do nothing but stunt their attempts at success, both personally and professionally. All children, from the earliest ages, are naturally inquisitive. They prefer to learn on their own terms. They persist in trying, despite warnings from their elders. Inquisitiveness is the sole reason for doing so. Try to remind yourself that your child will solve a problem depending on how they view it. Their way, just because it isn't what you would do, may not necessarily be wrong. Keep your eyes and heart open and watch them learn before jumping in to show them the "right" or "acceptable" way to solve an issue.

Children know when you are exhibiting an uncharacteristic urge to control them because of an underlying anxiety. They can pick up on cues and they learn to think if they can't reign in their natural behaviors, something bad will happen. It goes to show that nervous people raise nervous children. Therefore, try to understand how anxiety can come in the way of influencing your decisions and the ways in which you parent. Anxiety is difficult because it doesn't come with a conscious off-switch. It can run a mile without you realizing when you've gone in too deep and said things that you now regret. If your anxiety is overwhelming and you have tried mindfulness and boundary setting on your own without success, it may be time to talk to a mental health professional. Your stress management strategies should be tailored to your individual requirements, and a therapist can help you do just that. Your kid, who watches and mimics your every move, will learn how to handle stressful circumstances the same way if you can model resilience for them.

An overbearing parent will always teach their children that mistakes are the worst things to exist in the world. Yet, mistakes are indispensable tools for learning and growth. They help a child understand that the world itself is programmed to make individuals stumble and get up multiple times— and this is the only way to transition from just existing, to existing with resilience, confidence, and joy. If you are unable to let go of enough control to allow your kid to make errors, they will prob- ably internalize this message and look for ways to hide their own. Encourage your kid to learn from their errors. Reinforce the value of taking responsibility for one's actions and demon- strate that it's okay to miscalculate, so long as they pause and get to the bottom of why something didn't work out as they'd originally hoped it would (you included).

Finally, children who have controlling parents can develop mental health issues. Depression and anxiety are both the results of seeking absolute obedience. Children who cannot express themselves also become reticent and lack the ability to act with confidence as they transition to adulthood. Caregivers are the people children turn to for advice and emotional support. Parents must be understanding of their children's developmental stages and emotional requirements in order to help them through difficult emotional circumstances. This improves children's emotional and physical health, fosters stronger social interactions, and contributes to their academic and professional success when they grow up and face more difficult circumstances on their own. Research has revealed helicopter parenting, a style where parents are excessively focused on their children, can severely impact the child's ability to manage their emotions and behavior. They may be ill-equipped to deal with the changing demands of growth or be unprepared to navigate complex social environments. There-fore, they can act out in classrooms, struggle in school, and have a lot of difficulty in making friends.

Emotion and behavioral regulation are skills that all chil-dren must learn, and over-controlling parents can limit these opportunities. A particularly interesting piece of research studied four hundred and twenty-two children spread over eight years, assessing them at the ages of two, five and ten. The aim of the study was to look at the children's social and emotional development. In the observational phase, the research team told the children and their parents to play as they normally would in a home setting. They observed that some parents immediately resorted to helicopter parenting. They constantly guided their children by telling them what to play with, the correct way to play with a toy, how to clean up after themselves, and were just very demanding in general. Children responded by becoming apathetic, listless, angry, or frustrated (Kelly 2020).

The effects of over-controlling the child at the age of two was found to lead to poor emotional and behavioral manage-ment at the age of five. Also, they found that those who were allowed to develop their own voices and learn tools to cope had better social skills and were more productive at the age of ten. Children of supportive parents who did not micromanage them had better control over their impulses and were far less likely to engage in socially disruptive behavior patterns (Kelly 2020).

The best way for parents to teach their children self-control is by open communication about how they feel, what causes those feelings, and the possible outcomes of various reactions. Then, parents may guide their kids in developing healthy coping mechanisms, such as taking a few deep breaths, playing soothing music, drawing, or going into a quiet room by themselves. Parents may teach their children healthy ways to handle their own emotional responses in times of stress, by doing so themselves.

How To Find A Balance And Be Firm, Yet Loving As A Parent

Let's get one thing out of the way. Parenting is among the toughest, if not the most difficult, tasks you will undertake in this life. We examined the pitfalls of two kinds of parenting. The first, permissive or pushover parenting, is one where you basically think, "Whatever you need, just let me live in peace." The second, which is the domineering, authoritarian parenting, is "The parent's way or the highway." Now would be a good time to pause and ask yourself whether you lean more toward permissive or authoritarian parenting— are you more firm, or do you believe in teaching through friendship? There can also be a difference in the styles adopted by your partner and you. They may be a tough cookie, and you may be as soft as room-temperature butter. The best thing to do, of course, is to meet in the middle. There are benefits to taking the good things from each of the two approaches to establish a balanced middle ground.

A firm parent (who is authoritarian) lets kids know what is expected of them, both within and outside the home. Children know that they're dealing with someone they can't fool, so they remain likely to follow instructions and respect authority. This is only if the authority is balanced, not so excessive that children begin obeying less out of respect and more because they are afraid. A friendly parent, on the other hand, helps a child feel comfortable in their own skin. They feel free to explore themselves. They encourage their children to approach them with the smallest to the biggest of questions, therefore keeping their curiosity alive. They also strive to build a more authentic, genuinely loving relationship with their children outside of the obvious power-play in their relationships.

We want our children to be themselves, learn, have fun, but achieve all these wonderful things within a predetermined set of boundaries. We desire them to approach us with their problems and heartaches and be curious, but also pay attention when we are talking to them. They should look at us and not only know we love them, but also that we are deserving of their respect. In other words, we want a *balance*. This can happen once you move away from being a pushover and an authoritarian parent, come to the middle between the two, and learn the basics of *authoritative parenting*. The parents who adhere to this style believe in being firm and friendly. They view their children as individual people who need understanding, empathy and independence. In the same breath, they also know their roles lie in setting and enforcing boundaries, and encouraging their children to grow within the limits of these boundaries. Therefore, they raise children who:

- Are mindful of the consequences of their actions on others.
- Have confidence in themselves and their ability to grow.
- Share a deep love and mutual respect with their parents.

In the home, your effort to parent in an authoritative style means you will find balance between the need for your children to be their noisy selves, and also getting them to respect your request for a bit of peace and quiet. Before telling them off for being noisy, ask yourself, "Who should compromise right now?" You know your kids deserve room to just be their terrorizing selves— *all children do that.* That doesn't mean you have to tolerate pandemonium in the house 24/7. If you're sure you could all do with a bit of peace and quiet, go to their room, set up something that will engage them— an interactive puzzle or an audiobook could work wonders. Ask them to play in their room for a while, and take a timeout for yourself before the family comes together for a meal.

It'll take some time and a few trials before you have a system in place. The adversity of parenting is well-known. But then again, it is just as rewarding. The best way to teach your children what is and is not acceptable conduct is via consistent and fair discipline and consequences. Your children will learn what is and is not appropriate behavior based on how consistent you are with them and whether or not both of their parents use the same methods and guidelines. Make sure your partner and you are on the same page, and in time, you will get right where you need to be-- as a parent and an independent individual who can take pride in how stable their children are.

Of course, it goes without saying that children will keep running into issues from time-to-time as they navigate through life. This deserves a bit of a discussion. Let's get into it in the next chapter!

Chapter 10

Consciously Solving Problems That Arise

"Every day in a hundred small ways our children ask us, 'Do you see me? Do you hear me? Do I matter?' This behavior often reflects our response."

L.R. Knost.

C hildren are paradoxical creatures. There will be days you'll be completely convinced they are the most angelic beings in existence, only to find, in the very next hour, that their behaviors are verging on what can only resemble utter chaos. Whether you are dealing with a hyperenergetic, or strong-willed, or a subtle, clever child, every kid has certain idiosyncrasies that will show up at one point of time or the other. The manner in which you respond to their issues will also influence whether they repeat them in the future, and the degree to which these repetitions occur.

. . .

Lying

When I think of problems and children, the first one that comes to my mind is lying. Children can lie for any one of three reasons— they want attention, they're trying to get out of a tough spot, or they want to feel good about themselves. It helps to know which reason is pertinent to what you are dealing with because your course of action will be influenced by this. One way to arrive at the truth would be to look for nonverbal cues. Are their eyes shifty, or are they avoiding making eye-contact? Do you notice their hands trembling or their tone sounding nervous? You could also ask them something along the lines of, "Is that what happened, or do you wish that's how it would have happened."

Always make sure that telling the truth is an established and necessary household rule. If it is broken, there are consequences. If your children speak the truth, irrespective of how simple or difficult it may be for them, always praise them for choosing honesty. If they lied about scoring higher than they did on a test, for example, and eventually confessed, say something like, "I'm so proud that you were brave enough to tell me the truth. It can't have been easy. I have to take your *insert something they love and do every day* this evening, but I promise to return it to you tomorrow because you were honest."

Defiance

The next issue is defiance. If your child ignores you when you ask them to clean up after themselves or openly says "no" when you ask them to stop doing something annoying, it's difficult to not want to erupt in flames. Defiance stirs irritation in all of us, but it is in the nature of children to test our limits. If you give in, you give up. Limits are necessary and desired by preschoolers, so establish them and ensure your child understands them. Be explicit with your statements because this will give them boundaries. "We don't ever hit anyone. If you want something, either ask, or write it down." or, "You will always hold my hand before we cross the road, even if you are angry with me. You can be angry once we have finished crossing."

Tantrums And Aggression

Bedtime struggles are frequent, whether your youngster resists going to bed or wants to sleep with you. Your child might get sleep deprivation if you don't do anything. Lack of sleep has been linked to a variety of medical ailments. Create a schedule for going to bed, stick to it, and set firm bedtime limits. Consistency is the key to helping children develop good sleeping habits. You should keep sending your child back to bed, even if you have to do it a hundred times in an hour. They'll get better at going to bed on their own eventually.

It's possible that your issue involves a fussy eater. Or maybe your kid is sneaking food at inappropriate times. It's vital to tread cautiously when dealing with food-related habits, since they may lead to power battles and body image concerns. To raise children who have a positive relationship with food, parents should take preventative measures. Tell your kid that eating is for fueling their body, not for making them feel better or passing the time when they're bored or upset. Describe the many ways in which nutritious meals like veggies and whole grains may be delightful. Limit snacking and focus on serving one nutritious meal each day. Avoid using moral connotations on food like "veggies are good for you" or "this is healthy." Children relate to colors and vibrancy over health, which is still a concept they are learning to understand.

It's crucial to establish clear limits with children, just as it is with adults. Use concrete examples and take the time to fully explain the significance of each limit you set. Make an effort to observe your preschooler in positive situations as well as those when they are struggling. The little things you say to your kid, like "Thank you for being so tidy and cleaning all the toys from the bedroom!" or "It's so nice whenever you share with your baby sister!" may go a long way toward encouraging them to do more of the same. When praising your child, try to be as descriptive as possible, and highlight his or her effort rather than the final result.

If your kid is engaging in undesirable behavior, you may be compelled to scold them harshly, but before you do, consider the consequences of your words. Make sure your remarks are directed towards the kid's actions and not against the youngster themselves. Phrases like "You're so sloppy!" or "You're constantly getting in trouble" should be avoided. Also, remember that disciplining your disobedient 4-year-old is not the same thing as dominating them. Basically, you have to show them how to exercise self-discipline. Discipline should not be seen as a kind of punishment but rather as a means of instilling in your child the knowledge of right and wrong that will be necessary for them to become contributing members of society.

Screen Time

Another common behavioral problem with children could have to do with proper limits to screen-time. Your child may start shouting and throwing a tantrum whenever you ask them to turn the TV off, or they may even take your phone to play games when you aren't looking. You know an overload of screen time isn't healthy, so establish clear rules right at the onset.

When your kid disobeys your rules, it's time to set a good example by taking away their gadgets. Set up regular digital detoxes for the whole family to see how well everyone copes without technology.

Children may whine when they're not getting what they want. This will hurt, but the best first step is to often ignore it. Your intention is to show them that whining isn't going to get you to change your mind. When they stop, give positive attention and show you appreciate their mature responses. In time, also teach your children to handle uncomfortable emotions like disappointment. If they feel sad about not getting to watch cartoons at nine at night, it is far healthier to acknowledge the sadness over constantly whining about what they're unable to do. Expressing sadness gives them room to handle the emotion, and move to the reason for its existence— perhaps the sadness is because they have a cold, which is why they must rest at home. This gives their reasoning skills a boost. It also helps them understand and communicate with themselves before they jump to conclusions.

Impulsivity

Young children can be very impulsive, because this is the time when they are learning what emotions are and discovering the extremes— which, in time, will help them learn to tone their expressions. At this age, it's not unusual for kids to lash out or hit others in the attempt to get what they want. Set clear boundaries in place and reinforce, over and over, that it is okay to use words or scribble in a journal when your child feels angry, but taking the anger out on someone else by physically hurting them is not admissible. Every time they make the mistake of hitting someone, give them a timeout and ask them to think of what would happen if they were in the offended person's shoes. Also acknowledge when they apologize, or show their anger through words instead of hitting someone.

The Keys To Radical Love

So, what we want to encourage here is radical love. We use this to speak of a love that is forgiving, that exists as a whole and complete end unto itself. It is not fractured in expression or experience. In other words, it is the act of loving another being unconditionally. It is love that does not change, even if circumstances might. Don't make the mistake of thinking this labels you as a pushover. Unconditional love is not the same as "consenting" or allowing access unconditionally. Even if you need to separate yourself from someone because of your mental health, you can love them unconditionally from a distance.

This doesn't mean you are enabling them or giving them access to hurting you. It just means you are waiting and watching, and hoping they will find a way to the light. Naturally, parenting is one the most important domains that encourages radical love. Our children face immense mental damage when conditional love, dependent on them fulfilling our ambitions and expectations, is seen as the norm. If this is done, it can lead to anxiety, depression, or lifelong trauma. When it comes to parenting, radical love is providing affection without conditions or prerequisites. You keep the well-being of your child's mind and heart above your own, no matter what challenges you may be facing.

That doesn't mean parents should never correct their children; what's important is how they're disciplined. For example, if your kid has slapped someone, conditional love may lead you to emphasize the negative and convey the idea that your child is wrong. On the other side, those who love unconditionally seek to instill in their loved ones an understanding of the errors in their ways. It's looking at the act and behavior as wrong, not the entire child. One of the most important components of radical love in parenthood and family life is having patience, love, acceptance of oneself and others, and perspective to see things clearly.

Key One: Protecting Privacy

Teaching your kids to value privacy is something that will help both you and them as they enter their adolescent years. Parents are responsible for guiding their offspring through birth, childhood, adolescence, and beyond. Parents don't often realize that preparing their kids for adulthood requires giving them opportunities to hone and perfect the independence skills that will be essential to their success. Part of growing up and being ready to fly the coop is learning how and when to utilize privacy responsibly. Having more and more alone time will provide your adolescent the space they need to mature and acquire crucial skills.

When teenagers get the privacy they require, they become more independent and self-reliant. As a parent, always work to reach a balance between having the knowledge of what your teen is up to, believing they have what it takes to handle and also deserve a measure of privacy, and knowing that some situations will need you to step in. Trust your instincts, but give them the benefit of the doubt if their requests are within reason. This will depend upon a lot of factors— the safety of your neighborhood, the school environment, your child's temperament and needs, and the overall comfort levels shared by different members of your family. All in all, aim to make sure there is a measure of harmony.

Teenagers confront significant obstacles as they mature, such as figuring out what kind of individual they desire to be, where they belong socially, and what they wish to accomplish with their lives. They are acquiring new thinking abilities and establishing new interests in interpersonal, romantic, functional, and professional life, while their brains are also quickly growing. This period of time may also be a challenging transition for the parents. When it comes to your adolescent, there are, after all, a great many things that are unknown, and this may be unnerving. It is not always easy to let go, particularly if you have the impression that the other person is becoming farther away from you or if you are concerned that they may make decisions that are not in their best interests.

However, it is essential to keep in mind that just because your kid requests more solitude, this does not always indicate that they have anything to conceal from you. On the contrary, this is a normal and necessary aspect of the identity development process. Offering your child privacy is a way to let them know you trust them to make good choices. The more you show them you believe in their abilities, the less likely they will be to do things that will hurt your relationship (Ginsburg 2011). With this being said, always be watchful. You are a parent, which pretty much means you will never be off duty when it comes to vigilance. Be ready to step in if they display any signs of distress or repeatedly break your trust or the boundaries that you have set to their privacy.

Key Two: Listening Without Judging

First off, think of the kind of person you'd want your child to be once they grow up. Would you like them to pass comments and snide remarks whenever someone else shares something deeply personal with them? Or would you like them to be empathetic and compassionate people who will always be open to learning more about the other person's situation, even if it is beyond their understanding? If you chose the latter option, remember that children begin modeling parental behaviors from an early age. So, if you want them to be understanding people when they grow up, model that behavior and REALLY listen to what they're saying NOW. Listening to your child will help them develop a bond with you and solidify their trust in you being their safe space. When you communicate with your child, try to:

- Give non-verbal cues like nodding your head, keeping your eyes compassionate, and making the appropriate sounds. Encourage your child to talk with you.
- Be patient and listen without interrupting your child when they put their thoughts and feelings across.
- Once they have finished speaking, respond in a way that will mirror their thoughts and worries. Respond sensitively to what they say, the good and the bad.
- Focus on their body language and look for signs— do they look agitated, calm or happy? Can you notice any alterations in the way they speak with you and how they communicate with others around them? Are they quieter than usual? These are all signs something may be going on below the surface that deems your attention.

Listening without judgment is not a simple feat. There will be occasions when you will feel the obligation to voice your opinion and tell your kid they are wrong. Your youngster may say something that questions your position or ideas, or you may hear something that will make you want to change, or it may upset what you believe. That's why it's crucial to work on your own listening skills before you can expect your kid to open up to you. It takes a lot of patience to genuinely hear someone out, much less a kid, since you may get to hear a lot of things that you won't agree with or that won't make sense to you--including subjects that may involve the safety or wellbeing of your children. Whenever these topics do come up, remember the golden rule. First, let them speak. Hear them out. Offer your help once they have finished, and let them come to a conclusion based on this help, rather than making an all-out decision on their behalf. Here are some pointers to help you along the way:

- Engage in active listening by focusing on what the child is saying without expressing any opinions.
- Look at the situation from their perspective, and think of how you'd react if you were in their shoes.
- Be present, both physically, as well as mentally. Don't let your mind wander to a hundred different responsibilities that may be waiting for you. For now, let the world wait until you have finished communicating with your child.
- Have an open mind and be curious. Show interest in getting to know your child's perspective, and why they think as they do. When you do this, you will also be able to show them more conducive ways of rewiring thought patterns if and when necessary.

Key Three: Damage Control

There will be moments when your children will act in ways that make you upset. They'll drive you crazy, make you feel guilty even when you are trying your best. Whenever they behave in unreasonable ways— whining, crying, complaining or screaming— they are telling us we're falling short of something they want in the immediate moment. And it hurts, because that's the last thing you want. We think *they're thinking* we only neglect them, we don't give them what they want from us, and maybe we're not doing this entire parenting thing right. So, it becomes a toxic cycle where we're allowing one incident to open up a well of regret in us.

In turn, when we're guilty, we become more defensive. We feel compelled to lose our tempers or react with discomfort— which won't help our children at all. We begin snapping and forcing them to see why their feelings are wrong and why we're doing something that they don't like. In doing so, we forget that they're not bothered with looking at our justifications— they just want something which they won't get, and our shouting at them isn't going to make it any better. So they scream harder, and we feel more guilty.

That's the cycle.

How do we exit it?

Well, we do it by understanding that our feelings are leaving direct imprints on our children. When we think we have a "me" problem, the issue is that your child is also involved in the problem. And it's okay to feel guilty— but it's important to acknowledge that feeling. Understand that when you are uncomfortable, angry, or happy, your children will react to the way you express your emotions, and then, their behavior will be a reflection of your own. Normalize this rather than going to that tricky "It's all my fault and I suck at this" plane of parenting. This brings me to the next key.

Key Four: Offering Support

The next time you feel overtaken by a spell of anger, pause and repair the situation by coming clean. Trust me, it will make you feel better than you'd have hoped. You tap into that higher part of yourself which truly believes that you can do better, you can rise above the insecurities that claim all of us. So, just tell your child you snapped at them, and you know they don't deserve that, so you are sorry. Keep boundaries in place, and when both of you have calmed down, reinforce those boundaries gently, but firmly.

If you snapped at them because they kept interrupting your me-time, let them know you're apologetic for taking your frustration out on them. They're not at an age where they can understand the value of solitude the way adults do. Once they are calm, let them know you love them and you are always there for them, but you need an hour or two to yourself so you can be the kind of parent they deserve. Let them know it's all for them. Carve out enough time with your children each day— time where you sit with them and do a lot of things or nothing at all. Revel in each other's company, enjoy the moment, and let them feel how deeply you love them. This is transient, but in all these moments, you are building futures. It's the small gestures that count.

Key Five: We're In It Together

Love and security are the two indispensable traits that will carry your children sailing into adulthood. When children feel cared for, they can focus on other traits like creativity and learning. Here are some ways to let them know you love them.

- Of course, listen to your child. Make sure they know you are interested in their thoughts. Put down any gadgets and devices and show genuine interest in what they have to say.
- Affirming your love for your child with words is crucial, but don't forget the importance of touch when it comes to fortifying your relationship with your kids. Teenagers, in particular, still want tactile reassurance even if they no longer come rushing begging for it. Try to give them plenty of hugs every day.
- Even if you're not a fan of public shows of affection, there are other ways to show how much you care about someone. Put uplifting notes in their lunch boxes, give them high fives and compliments, and speak positively about them to others. The amount of concern that you have shown for them via your actions will tell them everything they need to know. Little things you do for them can go a long way toward making them feel appreciated.
- Have fun with each other. Play games, go on dates, be silly, just enjoy the happy days while also being there for each other during the difficult ones. Allow for enough flexibility, because unstructured fun will reveal parts of your child's character that may surprise you.
- Make a fun routine— perhaps make your favorite cookies on the weekend, or cook a meal once every week, or go for a movie or a shopping date. Whatever you choose, make sure it is special for each child and will stay with them as a core memory well into adulthood.

- Take their input. Involving kids in decision-making, whether it's as little as choosing a takeout or as large as their thoughts on a potential move, shows that you respect and appreciate their thoughts. A sense of community and safety is fostered when children can realize they can make a difference. This is something that will play a huge role in enhancing their confidence.
- Make sure your home has a structure. There will be variations from time-to-time, but so long as they return to the known pattern, they will thrive. Children appreciate and revel in consistency, so set patterns and maintain them when it comes to:
- Bedtimes
- Wake-up times
- Mealtimes
- Playtimes
- Parent-and-child special time
- Homework schedules
- Other extra-curricular activities
- Be attentive to all your children. Honor their individual identities, and always avoid making comparisons between them. Each of them will have their unique pursuits and talents, so cherish their quirks and love them for the talented little beings that they are. Also make it a point to pay attention to each of them— keep ten to fifteen minutes aside, where you spend solo time with every single kid you have. This is important for developing a sense of healthy self-esteem.

Key Six: Taking The Right Action

Your children don't feel insecure or unsafe because you have emotions that you share, process, and overcome with them. They feel terrible when you purposely show you don't have emotions, get overwhelmed and implode, or tell them that it's their fault you're experiencing anger and distress. It's no one's fault. Least of all theirs. Demonstrate and name your feelings using "I" dialogue.

So:

- Instead of saying, "You're making me mad," say something along the lines of, "I feel very frustrated when toys are littered around the room. How do we work through this together?"
- Rather than saying, "You're hurting my feelings," you could say, "I feel sad when I am being shouted at, sweetie. Of course it's fine to have big feelings. But shouting hurts the other person's heart."

Here, we fall back onto Occam's Razor. The simplest solution is often the correct one, and nowhere is this truer than when it comes to learning the route to healthy emotional expression. You don't want extreme suppression, and you don't want extreme expression. What's left? *The middle ground.* A balanced state, where you talk about what you are feeling, take control of your feelings (while showing they are natural under the circumstances), *and show your child you're working through them* is the ideal solution.

Research has found children display better emotional understanding if their mothers teach them to freely acknowledge their emotions when they were three. The more the mothers talked, the healthier the outcome (Dunn, Brown, and

148

Beardsall 1991). Another study looked at the journals of mothers (containing emotional expressions) that they had shown their preschoolers. The journals included details of how the mothers had faced and coped with their emotions. The offspring of mothers who experienced sadness and pain (and described ways of coping with them) were found to have more emotional intelligence as well as greater prosocial behavioral skills (Denham and Grout 1992). Consider these three options:

- You are very depressed and must leave your room to cry. Your child can sense something is amiss, but doesn't know what it is.
- You are upset. You cry a little, and tell your child, "I've had a bad day, love. It's got nothing to do with you. But you know what? All I need to do is have dinner and talk to your father for a bit, and everything will be alright."
- You are so upset you can't stop crying in front of your child.

In the second scenario, you are expressing your emotions, and telling your child how you plan to deal with them. This is you being an emotional coach for them, and showing them how they can use negative emotions as problem-solving opportunities to learn and grow. The next time your youngster witnesses you cry, get upset, or get exasperated, try to put it in words they can understand. It's possible that you'd be helping them out. It could be beneficial to you as well. Little ones have hearts of gold and often provide sound counsel that is certain to bring unexpected lightness and joy.

Key Seven: Evaluate And Appraise

Many parents feel helpless when their children exhibit disruptive behavior. Perhaps you've experimented with several forms of discipline without much success. Children do best with clear, consistent limits, so using too many methods to curb misbehavior might be counterproductive. Even if you haven't noticed any changes yet, keep in mind that parents have more sway than they may imagine when dealing with defiant children. Improving kids' conduct and even the parent-child connection is possible with behavior management.

- Refuse to give up. Don't give in to your child's demands to terminate their tantrum. Their outbursts will be successful if you give in to them.
- Stay composed. Your youngster will learn positive conduct from seeing you remain calm. When children are met with harsh or emotional reactions, their verbal or physical aggressiveness tends to increase.
- Ignore the child's little misbehaviors, since any kind of positive or negative attention might reward the child's activities. On the other hand, provide specific labels when praise is given for desirable actions. For instance, when they calm down, say "Good job on calming yourself!"
- Use consistent measures of discipline. Your kid has to know that there are repercussions for bad conduct (like time outs) and incentives for good behavior (like story time).
- Put off your conversation till the outburst is done. When a youngster is distressed, it is best not to attempt to reason with them. You should teach

your kid to negotiate at calm moments, when they (and you) are less likely to explode.

In order to control disruptive behavior, it is important to first determine which actions you want to modify (or encourage). When everyone in a family is stressed out, it might seem like every conversation is an uphill battle. But the first step in implementing effective discipline is to pinpoint particular habits. Taking one habit at a time helps you concentrate, figure out why it's occurring, and feel more in charge of the situation. Misconduct is typically a result of these factors:

- Assuming your needs have been fully communicated: Even if you think a child knows what is expected of them, they may not. Children are more prone to act inappropriately when they are confused about the expectations placed on them, which occurs often since expectations vary depending on the context.
- Important instructions should not be called out from afar. Instead, provide them to your youngsters face to face. Orders screamed from afar are less likely to be heard and followed.
- Kids often find it challenging to adjust their activities in the midst of something they like doing when they are abruptly interrupted. Children's anxiety during transitions may be reduced if they are given advance notice and the opportunity to locate a safe halting spot.
- Making a series of inquiries or providing a list of directives: If you ask a group of kids a series of questions or give them a set of instructions, it's less likely that they'll pay attention to what you're

saying, remember what you want them to do, or follow your directions.

Finally, here's what you can do to encourage positive results in future.

- Take care of the mental and physical stresses that make it harder for kids to control their conduct.
- Consider factors like hunger, exhaustion, worry, and other potential interruptions. For instance, during homework time, parents should limit the use of electronic devices, set up a quiet, clutter-free work space, stock it with healthy foods, and plan for regular breaks.
- Set clear expectations that allow both you and your kid to thrive.
- Preparing youngsters for imminent changes by providing countdowns. If you want her to come to supper or start her schoolwork, for instance, give her a 10-minute heads-up. As soon as there are two minutes remaining, follow up. Making the change at the specified time is as crucial as sending the countdown.
- It's crucial for teenagers to have some control over their timetables. The simple act of offering a structured option, such as "Do you want to take a shower after supper or before?" may help children feel in control and motivate them to develop better self-regulation skills.

At the end of the day, the best things will happen when you discipline in a manner that helps your children learn. Yes, you want to shield them, but not at the cost of them learning to develop their own identities. It's not the mistakes that are the issues— it's failing to learn from them. So, whenever they make an error or a miscalculation, resist the urge to step in and save the day. Let them come to terms with what has happened, but also encourage them to think of solutions and figure a way around whatever issue they are facing. Chances are, both you and they will be proud of just how far you go in the process. The truth is simple. Your children will grow up. They will make their choices, stumble, and if you love them well, they will rise once more, stronger than ever. So, in the next chapter, we will talk about ways for you to lovingly accept their kids for who they are.

Chapter 11

Accepting And Loving Your Child

"Making the decision to have a child is momentous. It is to decide forever to have your heart go walking outside your body."

Elizabeth Stone.

I'd be outright lying if I said I got into parenting without the picture of what my ideal child would look like. I envisioned all of it— but most of all, I wanted a baby that would love me for who I was, with all of my flaws and imperfections. The truth is, there will be a lot of deviations from the image you have in your head. Maybe their eye color won't be as blue, or the extroversion you expected isn't there, and your child is a complete introvert. However, even with all the changes and the things that didn't turn out the way you'd expected they would— one aspect remains unequivocally certain. Your children will learn how to love from you.

And they will love you with no conditions attached. So, if they can do that— you can as well. We would do anything to keep our children happy, but then again, we often find ourselves caught in a web of confusion and disagreements when we don't agree with letting them become the kind of people they aspire to be. Perhaps our ideals or expectations from them were different. Whenever such discord strikes, it's important to know you didn't give birth for yourself. We mistake the act of reproduction as an extension of ourselves in a new physical body. What we're actually doing is creating a whole new life. And every form of life will have its own characteristics. The best, and most graceful thing to do is to accept them and watch them flourish.

Support Your Children And Their Passions

Sensitive responses to your kid may not come easy, particularly if you were raised by a parent who was harsh or inattentive. It may take some time before you feel certain you have a firm grasp of your child's requirements and how to best meet them. A newborn lacks the coping mechanisms necessary to deal with stress. As they are soothed and comforted by a caretaker, they gradually learn how to handle difficult emotions. It's crucial to react quickly to a baby's screams and needs, especially when they're younger.

- Thinking about what your face, voice, body, words, and thoughts need to express in order for your kid to feel safe and secure will help you react sensitively to your child.
- If a face could show emotion, what expressions would it make? Make plenty of calm eye contact with your kid to show that you care. Replicating their expressions is also useful.
- Use a voice that is neither too loud nor too quiet, but rather soothing and kind.

- You may assist in calming your kid by physically holding them while they're upset. Remaining calm in body language is another way to reassure your youngster. Comforting touches like hugs and rocking may also make a difference.
- Speak softly, kindly, and encouragingly, particularly while under pressure. Your kid will feel better if you address them by their name, explain what's going on, and explain how they could be feeling.

One helpful strategy is to have an open line of communication with your kid and to set reasonable limits on what you expect from them. When a caretaker is attentive to a child's needs, the child gains invaluable experience and knowledge. Youngsters pick up on the message that they are important and appreciated. They gain lifelong skills in emotional regulation as they work through adversity. Ultimately, they find out that they can rely on you to ease their worries whenever they need it. Feeling good about yourself as a parent and your connection with your kid may be bolstered by knowing that you are facilitating your child's healthy growth and development.

Your priority as a parent is protecting your kid and setting them up for success. What they need is:

- An environment where basic needs are prioritized, including a secure and healthy place to live, nutritious food, and school materials
- To know they are loved and to have confidence that they will always have your support
- Consideration of their needs and emotions
- Respect for their friends, wardrobe, sports, music preferences, and hobbies, as well as appreciation

for significant life events, such as birthdays or the first day of school.

Some parents have a hard time adjusting to the increased obligations of raising a teenager. This is a moment when even the most solid and loving bonds may be tested. Your kid needs you now in a different manner than in the past, but no less.

They're counting on you to help them through one of the most challenging times as they transition into adulthood and learn to rely on themselves. You understand how frustrating and complicated it may be since you've been there. Don't be shy about telling your child about your own adolescent trials and tribulations. Try assuring them that you can relate since it also occurred to you. Share your thoughts on how you dealt with the situation and what you learned from it. A youngster might get great comfort in hearing from their parent that other people have similar difficulties. Your kid is maturing into their own person. They need ideals and standards that will serve as a guide now and as they grow up. Think about how you want to instill your family's beliefs and expectations in your kid. In this manner, kids will be equipped with the information necessary to make choices in accordance with the family's core beliefs and successfully navigate the world on their own.

The adolescent years will undoubtedly be a time of increased anxiety and annoyance. If you're a parent, you've probably had moments when you felt on the outside looking in or were disappointed in your child's decisions. Be there for them through every difficulty, big or little, with as much love and support as you can muster. If you can accomplish this, they'll be more inclined to trust you, confide in you, and turn to you for assistance during tough times.

Your child's healthy growth and your relationship may benefit greatly from certain adjustments in your approach to parenting. In the same way you hoped your own parents would always be there for you, be that parent for your child. Keep in mind that it's never too late to treat your kids with the respect and care they deserve.

Keep Communication Channels Open

Look for creative ways to get your child to communicate with you. This will build a climate where they feel good, regardless of whether they talk about little or big things. Don't wait for something huge to happen before you begin speaking with your child. Communicate about routine, trivial things that happen everyday— look for different opportunities that signal to you. It's crucial to start up a dialogue with your children in a way that doesn't make them feel threatened. Inquiring about your child's day without coming off as intrusive is a great approach to foster conversation and get a sense of how things are going in his or her world.

Direct queries may be seen as frightening by your kid and may drive them to withhold information, so be gentle. It's not an interview, after all. Always pay attention when they're telling you something. It took a few repeated "You're not listening to me!" exclamations to help me realize how important listening skills were. Remember they are looking up to you, and when they share, they are pouring their whole hearts out. If your kid needs to speak to you about anything and you're too busy to pay attention, schedule a time when you can. When kids believe we're not paying attention to what they're saying, they often stop trying to communicate with us.

One thing that has really helped me is to be specific with my questions. If I ask something vague, like— did you like school today? I'm not really giving them a chance to voice anything, because by attaching "like'" to my question, I'm forcing them to just say "yes" or "no." It's not an open-ended question. Instead, I ask something like, "What was the best part about school today? And what didn't you like so much?" This gives them a broader platform to share whatever has gone on with their day, and to let me know if something has troubled them. I can also take it a step further to help them find solutions to whatever they didn't like, using a "what" and "if" approach.

So, I'll ask something on the lines of "If you could change this, what would you do?" I even use magic at times, because hey, it's adorable when their faces light up with faith. "What if a fairy comes at night and grants you a wish to change something about your day? What would you choose to change?" If your child is very young, make sure they look at the act of communicating as a game— this will teach them that they never need to be afraid when they are sharing something with you. Pretend to put on a pair of "listening ears" and tell them you're under a spell, which means now, they have your undivided attention. Start conversations and be happy when they talk gibberish and take you on one of their imaginary journeys. We have much to learn from the imagination of a child, so revel in it.

Accept Their Friends

Be open to inviting your children's friends over. See whether they can handle living in your house with your set of rules. Make sure your child's peers understand and can follow your family's standards, such as using appropriate language and asking for permission before eating. If your kid has chosen a friend who is causing you stress, you may learn from this, whether you should be encouraging or diverting this connection. Participate in your children's school, sporting, or club activities, if you have the time. Some preteens may prefer that you remain unseen so as not to humiliate them, but it's best to be there nevertheless. Preteens in these situations may not pay you much attention, if any attention at all. Here is your opportunity to see your kid in action and witness firsthand how they interact with their classmates.

One of the finest ways to encourage positive actions in your adolescent is to develop relationships with the families of their peers. Keep in mind that during teenage years, children worry about being "accepted" within the larger circle. They want to be "cool" and do things that will show they're normal, and they may make risky choices in an effort to show they are normal, or that they fit in within the accepted and popular social rubric. They may act out if they are subjected to more stringent rules than their peers. However, when parents collaborate to establish shared norms, teenagers are less likely to believe they are being singled out and more likely to follow the rules without hesitation.

This goes without saying— always honor their requests. If your child is calling you to a show, or a play, or an open house, or whatever it is, it means they trust and love you and want you present as a form of support. Every time you say you can't make it, you push them further and further away. This leaves room for hurtful feelings and they also tend to make wrong associations because the emotion of being "unloved" can propel all human beings to seek validation elsewhere. You want them to look at you and think, "This is someone who'll be there for me through all my highs and lows. They'll cheer for me no matter what." One sureshot way to this is to just be present. When they grow up, they should be able to look back on the memories of their school events and remember how you were always there for them.

Be Artful About Your Disapproval

This one can be a bit of a doozy. It's hard not to experience anger, guilt, and resentment as your children grow up, hit puberty, and repeatedly engage in those very behaviors that you spent so much time teaching them not to do. They may make poor decisions, associate with those who aren't right for their best interests, spend too much money, refuse to listen to reason, or just reign hell in the house, because that's what teenagers do. They're going through a difficult time, and they may think the only way to counter that is to inflict their rage on everyone around them. A time may come when you begin questioning yourself— *Where did I go wrong? How could the baby who was so sweet have grown up to make such bad decisions? How can they not see it's affecting us?* It's so tempting to swoop in and help them— but wait.

Take a deep breath, and prepare yourself for a conversation with your child. Process your own emotions beforehand so you can be as stoic as possible— although you may be on fire from the inside. Be mindful of what needs to be said, because this cannot come across as a lecture or an interrogation. Don't fix the issue for them. Ask what they are trying to accomplish, show your concern, and offer your wisdom. Suggest some people they can take help from, or even tell them where they can access useful resources, but let them come to a solution by themselves.

Of course, you will do whatever you can to ensure that your child has all the resources they need to grow up into competent adults. In the next chapter, we will discuss this in greater detail. Yet, if there are times they fail to live up to the pedestals we do involuntarily place them on, understand that it's okay to be sad. The ups and downs of parenting an adult kid who keeps making bad choices may be exhausting. You'll feel like you're making headway one day, only to find yourself back at square one the next. It's tempting to give in, but resist the urge. Try talking things through with a trustworthy, experienced friend or going to therapy. Cry your eyes out, give voice to your hurt, rage, and figure out how you will work through whatever has come to pass.

Chapter 12

Raising Thriving Kids

"My father didn't tell me how to live; he lived, and let me watch him do it."

Clarence Budinton Kelland.

Right from the time they are tiny, children will surprise you with the tremendous rate at which they can grasp new skills. To thrive, they need to trust their judgment and capabilities, while also knowing it's okay not to be successful at everything. At the very onset, we aim to help our children acquire essential life skills to help them deal with problems logically and healthily. These skills include honing creativity, finding solutions via critical thought, cooperating and communicating with others, and developing awareness, independence, and social and personal responsibility. By the age of twelve, children should be able to

- Follow a daily routine.

- Bathe alone and be mindful of their hygiene.
- Choose their own outfits.
- Participate in household chores like folding clothes, doing laundry, helping in the kitchen, preparing the dinner table, making the bed, cleaning up after themselves, and responding to your calls for help.
- Learn the essentials of saving money and spending wisely.

Cultivate Your Children's Talents

Young people benefit from branching out into new areas of interest rather than concentrating only on those in which they currently excel. Developing one's skill set gives children a sense of agency and the assurance that they can take on any challenge. It's human nature to want to shield your child from disappointment. Still, kids learn best via trial and error, and seeing their efforts fall short teaches them that it's okay to try again. It may also motivate children to work more, serving them well. It's crucial to learn how to persevere through adversity and keep going when things become tough. Confidence and self-esteem do not depend on always being the greatest at everything; instead, they stem from a willingness to keep trying despite setbacks. Kids' self-assurance and sense of self benefit from their time to discover and pursue their hobbies. As a natural byproduct, seeing their abilities improve will also do wonders for their sense of pride in themselves. Children develop confidence when they set and achieve both major and minor objectives.

Encourage your kid to write down their aspirations so that they may begin working toward them. Next, get in the habit of chunking your long-term objectives into more manageable milestones. By doing so, you'll validate their passions and provide them with the tools they'll need to succeed in the long run. While it's fantastic to congratulate children on their successes, it's just as vital to let children know that you're happy with their efforts, win or lose. Demonstrate your admiration for the efforts of children of all ages, from babies constructing with blocks to teens learning to play an instrument independently. Developing a new talent requires time and effort, and the payoff can take time and effort. Urge them to take part. Children, despite their grumbling, benefit socially and emotionally when given age-appropriate responsibilities, such as helping with household chores or transporting younger siblings home after a play date.

Being wanted by your family is more significant than doing your homework or participating in after-school activities. Children must learn that attaining perfection is impossible at a young age. Teach your children that the idealized version of the world they see on television, in magazines, and on their friends' social media feeds is a dangerous delusion. Instead, reassure them that imperfections are human and acceptable. Children benefit from challenges, but also need chances to try things where they have a strong chance of succeeding. Involve your kid in something that will help them feel safe and confident, so they can take on more complex tasks. Give your kid assurance of your unwavering affection. Good or terrible, win or lose, pass or fail. Remember our reliance on radical love. Your child's sense of worth may be boosted even when they aren't feeling particularly good about themselves, if they know you think they're amazing all the time, not just when they accomplish fantastic things.

Teach Them Life-Skills Early On

The very first skill our children should learn is to make decisions on their own. Allow young children enough opportunities to make choices— what will they wear each day? What can they eat for a snack? When should they do their homework? Natural consequences— like choosing something unhealthy for a snack and then getting hungry too soon, or wearing airy clothes on a winter day, while painful to watch, will help reinforce the appropriateness of some choices over others. Children like to be in control and choose between different options rather than just being told what they must do. By elementary school, they will also decide who to have as friends, what kinds of activities they can participate in, and how they can spend their free time constructively. As they grow up, they should make wise choices on how to spend their money, who to go out with, and what paths to follow in terms of professional and academic pursuits. The more they learn about themselves through their decisions, the greater their self-assurance will be.

Foster a sense of independence. It will be easier for you to complete tasks for your children. It may also lead to cleaner results. But if we want our children to grow up to be confident and self-reliant people, we must provide them with the means to do so. They should have the self-discipline to do their homework, put their clothes away, and clean up after themselves. Give your kid the tools they need to succeed on their own and grow in self-confidence. By the age of thirteen, children should have developed enough independence, giving the opportunity to safely allow them to spend brief amounts of time alone at home.

Owning And Caring For A Pet

As well as benefiting the household and the pet, instilling in a youngster the responsibility and confidence that comes with taking on a job as challenging as pet care is a gift that keeps on giving. Let them be part of the selection process and reinforce that the pet is their responsibility. Help them realize your pet is a live being with a heart and a soul, and that their loyalty must be earned. Your youngster will need to understand why they are responsible for the pet's upkeep. You should talk to your kid quietly and in a calm setting, if you are introducing a new pet into the home, giving them more responsibility, or assigning them a domestic duty. Recognize that your kid will inevitably make some errors. But instruct children to treat their pets with dignity and to be firm when it comes to stopping bad behavior, like yanking the tail or lashing out. Learning love is best accomplished by tender means.

- Make the children a part of the selection process and choose a pet they can relate to.
- Help them understand the pet is a family member and will be one for life.
- Involve the children in preparing for the pet's arrival.
- Teach them to not disturb a pet when the pet is eating, drinking, or resting.
- Supervise over them while allowing them to learn to walk pets on a leash.
- Don't let your child punish a pet who has made a mistake. Never encourage this. They can have trouble reigning in abrupt lashings or retaliating with anger, so unless and until they are mature and calm in their actions, supervise their interactions.

- Don't let them feed table scraps or human food to the pets.
- Don't burden them with too many responsibilities surrounding the pet's upkeep. Only give what they can capably do and learn from.
- Don't punish your child by threatening to separate them from their pet.

Money Skills

When children are old enough to understand sticking pennies in their mouths isn't such a great idea, they're ready to learn about money. Explain what it is, what it can do, and how you can use it— by demonstration rather than in theory. Make purchases in front of them and show them how it works. Detail the structure of receipts whenever you take them shopping, and eventually, they will understand money is how they can buy things. Instill a habit of saving. It's important because they'll constantly watch you purchase things, including items for them. They must know that money is more than just spending — that the best rewards are reaped when one learns to balance income with expenditure to create a little nest egg for the future. Saving will help them become more disciplined and also get them to learn about delayed gratification. It will teach them about setting goals and planning, and help them be more prepared and secure in their ability to make wise choices. Provide your children with a piggy bank or other kind of savings container, so they may begin learning the value of saving at a young age. Then, encourage them with brief, straightforward remarks. I saw this wonderful series long back where people kept their money in little earthen pots that they'd break only when they deemed a purchase as satisfying three criteria— need, truly want, and further investment. The next time your kids come running up to you and say they want a particular video game, show them how they can save and buy it themselves.

Young people should have their own spending money so they may practice making responsible financial choices. A monetary stipend serves that purpose. But you might think about making your kids complete tasks in exchange for their stipend. In general, people place a higher value on their own earnings than on money they just get. Of course, they must do some tasks without pay because they're part of a house and have responsibilities to the family. But from time-to-time, encourage them to open lemonade stalls, watch someone else's pet, mow a lawn, rake leaves from a neighbor's yard, and do other such tasks for earning some money on their own.

Money management skills are vital to instill in your children, but so are the examples you set while they are around you. You are sending contradictory signals if, after complaining about how expensive resources can be, you then go on a spending spree with your children. Instead, be a role model for your children regarding money. If your children are to value a budget and save money wisely, they need to witness you doing the same. In other words, lead by example and be consistent in your preaching. Teaching your kids about money management is an ongoing effort. However, put in the time and effort to convey a cohesive message about finance. You will help your children develop healthy financial habits that will last a lifetime.

Cooking, Cleaning And Table Manners

This may be a battle at the start, but slowly and surely, get your children to participate in household chores. Having them help around the house can actually be rewarding. Choose tasks that are age-appropriate and always praise them for helping out. Some parents also give children an allowance upon completion of tasks— but giving money is not essential unless you want to teach them about financial responsibility.

Start with basic chores that will help all of you keep your home tidy and presentable. Keep a scorecard and a checklist for expectations regarding how the children should help out, and let them earn stickers— maybe even an extra few minutes of playtime— when they complete a task. Key tasks include putting their toys away, placing dirty clothes in the hamper, clearing dishes, feeding pets, washing dishes, sweeping, and vacuuming. Introduce your adolescent to the washing machine, the safe use of home cleaning solutions, refilling the gas tank, lawn mowing and assisting with other household tasks as they become older.

As your children grow up, allow them access to the kitchen, but make sure everything is safe and well-maintained. Don't give them any sharp objects until they reach their teenage years and have learned to be careful around different kitchen appliances. Let them watch you work in the kitchen, and if they ask questions about what you are doing, always participate and explain how cooking works. It's good to let them know where their food comes from, and why cooking at home is better than eating out. Wherever possible, introduce these concepts and also explain how nourishment works.

Before the age of five, you can encourage any curiosity in the kitchen by letting your children wash and "make" food alongside you. Keep a few unbreakable bowls, some water, and a couple of utensils handy. Teach them to make pretend "soups." Take their help in pouring ingredients into bowls. If it is safe, let them feel, explore, stir and taste what you cook with. Ask them what it smells like, how it tastes, and what should happen with it. Little kids love water, so if you can, teach them the basics of washing produce. In the kitchen, there are a few precautions that adults often overlook that should be drilled into children:

- Keep the handle facing away from you so you don't accidentally bump against it.
- Keep a dry dish cloth or a pot holder handy at all times for grabbing handles.
- To avoid burning your hands, keep the handles away from the heat sources.

Giving your children the opportunity to prepare a whole lunch on their own is a great way to teach them independence and responsibility. Having children help decide what to pack in their lunchbox is a great confidence booster, and it also increases the likelihood that the food will be consumed. This is a terrific opportunity to educate kids about the importance of including protein, fruit, veggies, and whole grains into their diets, as well as some of the basics of nutrition.

Preparing the table for dinner may be a responsibility that your child aged three to five will gladly take on. They may help set the table by folding the napkins and learning the proper placement of the cutlery. It's the same after eating. Permit them to collect the dishes and return them to the kitchen. Your kid will get a kick out of feeling useful while also relieving some of your burden. When they sit down to a meal, always reinforce some dining table etiquettes:

- Everyone comes to the table with clean hands and faces. Children will wash up before dinner, not just because it is a good hygiene practice, but also as a sign of respect for all diners.

- Wait until every single person at the table is served before eating. Meals are better when enjoyed together.
- Chewing with the mouth closed and refraining from talking with a full mouth.
- Eating with small bites and relishing each mouthful rather than wolfing the food down.
- Saying "please" when asking for a second serving, and "thank you" when they are given food on their plates.
- Help children learn that while they may not like something, they should never criticize food or what any other people eat. Also teach them to know the preparation and love that goes into making a meal out of ingredients, and the basic philosophy behind cultural food differences when they are old enough.

Safety And Security Skills

Learning how to provide first aid, as well as when and how to call for help, is a very useful ability. Emergencies don't usually come with a prior announcement, so our children need to know how to manage troublesome situations until help comes. Make sure your kid knows your actual name (as opposed to just 'mom' or 'dad), and where they live (all details of the address and any landmarks). They should also know the address of your work-space, and how to get in touch with you before letting them remain home alone. Disseminate information regarding the whereabouts and contents of any household first aid kits. Kids need to learn basic fire safety precautions as well as first aid skills like cleaning and bandaging.

It is imperative that you instruct your child in basic self-defense techniques, even if you hold out hope that they will never have to use them. The growing number of parents who are concerned about their children being abducted has contributed to an increase in the number of youngsters who participate in self-defense classes. Children have the ability to defend themselves and experience a greater sense of safety if they are taught fundamental self-defense methods such as strategies for verbally de-escalating potentially dangerous situations.

Whether you are concerned about your child being attacked by a random person on their route home from school or your adolescent has a job that necessitates them to be out late, teaching them how to use self-defense can give them the assurance they need to feel safe and put your mind at ease. Consider signing them up for local defense classes, or even get them a punching bag and a pair of good gloves. There are wonderful self defense and kickboxing videos on platforms like YouTube, fall back on them to teach your children how to defend themselves. If you'd like, join in and participate with them!

Sibling Care And Social Skills

Teaching kids to share is a terrific approach to instill a sense of community among them and will help them grow up to be kind, giving people. The more time they spend together, the more memories they make. But, be patient. This is something they will learn from you. It will need self-control and under-standing— particularly if you have a child who is an older sibling. They'll look at the younger ones and get frustrated thinking how they can make simple mistakes. If you can't show them what patience looks like and why it's so essential, they won't learn. Teach your children the joys of sharing. The best method to foster caring connections is via shared play. When kids play, they pick up crucial life skills like sharing and taking turns. They are bonding and learning about one another via shared enjoyment. It's certain that there will be near-catastrophic times when siblings play together, but that's when you, the parent, may step in and mediate.

Commencing from the preschool years, be present and available when your children go on playdates or spend time with other kids. You will be able to identify patterns about how your children interact with the world around them. Make note of their social strengths and the areas where they fumble. If they are shy, step in to help where you can, and if they are very outgoing, teach them to also understand the workings of quieter minds. Let their circle be diverse. Give them instruction on resolving and sharing different conflicts which won't involve getting into wrestling matches with one another. This is something we must take note of— even at very young ages, children do get angry with their friends. But with you being involved, you will have the opportunity to understand the conversations that make them angry, and how they tend to respond if they act on impulse. Teach them that anger is temporary and they should not ruin a good relationship because of a transient emotion or moment.

During their school years, don't adopt a complete "they must work it out by themselves" approach. In measure, it is true — they must learn to fend for themselves. But you can still support and model healthy friendships and teach them everyone deserves to have a good social support surrounding them. If your child is shy, encourage them to not respond to conflicts with increasing isolation. Let them know conflicts are temporary and if they truly like someone, the feeling will persist beyond the immediate issue. If your child has trouble focusing, take time to help them slow down and filter their thoughts before they express themselves too quickly or are overtly harsh. The same applies for a physically active child. Let them know that it is never okay to hurt others. Every child will need some skills to become adept at the web of social interactions. Make sure you're taking time to help them learn.

Personal Hygiene

Always emphasize good hygiene skills. Young children should be encouraged to take responsibility for their own personal grooming by learning to dress themselves, brush their teeth and face, wash their hair and body, and determine for themselves when they need to do laundry. Other aspects of personal hygiene, such as knowing when to start wearing antiperspirant, become more important for pre-teens and teenagers as they reach puberty. Keep good hygiene practices yourself, and they will follow suit.

* * *

By equipping children with practical life skills, you can send them out into the world with the assurance that they will be able to handle themselves. Make a conscious effort to teach children what is essential to adapt to life's changing seasons relatively easily. They will also rise to challenges, including navigating tricky situations like bullying. It will give them a voice they can rely on and allow them to develop the experiences they need to know their responsibilities and rights. There are some ways for you to ensure they take on tasks with confidence. For instance, model confidence, even if you don't feel up to it on some days.

When your children see you handle new tasks with optimism and preparedness, they get motivated to do the same. Acknowledge when you feel anxious, but show them how you navigate the anxiety and reach a helpful solution. Please don't be upset about mistakes; teach your children to learn from them instead of dwelling on them. Confident individuals don't allow the possibility of failure to stop them, not because they think they'll never fail, but because they've learned to bounce back quickly from disappointments.

Final Words

We are now at the end of our journey together. In these last few paragraphs, I want to remind you that children are among the most intuitive of all living beings. They pay attention. If you love others, you set up examples for them to follow. If you demonstrate negative behaviors, including fighting, displaying discord, always being grumpy or calling names, they will pick up on that too.

So, love abundantly and equally. If you have more than one child, demonstrate that each and every one of them matter the same to you. Help them realize that they can learn to be a team and enjoy the sibling experience without feeling jealous.

There are so many wonderful life lessons you will learn from your children. Most of all, perhaps, you will remember what it's like to view the world with a sense of child-like wonder and awe. The mere sight in their eyes when they discover something new, or find a solution to something by themselves, is enough to make you think, "Wow, look at them. They've unlocked the secrets to happiness and they're only three."

You will begin seeing little pieces of yourself in them. Maybe they'll laugh like you used to, or say things in the same tone and with similar vocalizations. They will remind you how precious life is over and again, and show you the privilege of shaping young minds is something you can claim all for yourself— if you are brave and compassionate.

I would say, above everything, embrace every minute of this wonderful experience. Cry over the lows, rejoice the highs, and love each second as deeply as you can. It is so fulfilling to watch your children grow up and take their places in the world, but it can be heartbreaking too.

The entire journey is like a kaleidoscope, at the end, you have a small instrument in your mind which only relays memories in sepia. You want these memories to be happy, to remind you of how much fun you had and what a time it was. This is you setting up a future— not just for your child, but yourself.

Make the journey worthwhile.

I hope you enjoyed accompanying me in this road to comprehending gentle parenting. If you liked the read, don't forget to leave a review on Amazon!

Sources

Bailey, Jennifer A., Karl G. Hill, Sabrina Oesterle, and J. David Hawkins. 2009. "Parenting Practices and Problem Behavior across Three Generations: Monitoring, Harsh Discipline, and Drug Use in the Intergenerational Transmission of Externalizing Behavior." *Developmental Psychology* 45 (5): 1214–26. https://doi.org/10.1037/a0016129.

Berman, Marc G, Ethan Kross, Katherine M Krpan, Mary K Askren, Aleah Burson, Patricia J Deldin, Stephen Kaplan, Lindsey Sherdell, Ian H Gotlib, and John Jonides. 2012. "Interacting with Nature Improves Cognition and Affect for Individuals with Depression." *Journal of Affective Disorders* 140 (3): 300–305. https://doi.org/10.1016/j.jad.2012.03.012.

Bredehoft, David J. 2021. "The Mental Health Consequences of Parental Overindulgence." Https://Www.Psychologytoday.Com/Us/Blog/the-Age-Overindulgence/202106/the-Mental-Health-Consequences-Parental-Overindulgence. June 8, 2021.

Carrell, Scott, Richard Fullerton, and James West. 2008. "Does Your Cohort Matter? Measuring Peer Effects in College Achievement." Cambridge, MA. https://doi.org/10.3386/w14032.

Clark, Beverly, and Beth Kurylo. 2010. "Children Benefit If They Know About Their Relatives, Study Finds."

Cuddy, Emily, and Richard v. Reeves. 2014. "Hitting Kids: American Parenting and Physical Punishment." Https://Www.Brookings.Edu/Research/Hitting-Kids-American-Parenting-and-Physical-Punishment/. November 6, 2014.

Denham, Susanne Ayers, and Leslie Grout. 1992. "Mothers' Emotional Expressiveness and Coping: Relations with Preschoolers' Social-Emotional Competence."

Diener, Edward, Richard E. Lucas, and Jorden A. Cummings. 2021. "Personality Traits ." In *Introduction To Psychology* . Creative Commons.

Dunn, Judy, Jane Brown, and Lynn Beardsall. 1991. "Family Talk about Feeling States and Children's Later Understanding of Others' Emotions." *Developmental Psychology* 27 (3): 448–55. https://doi.org/10.1037/0012-1649.27.3.448.

Durrant, Joan, and Ron Ensom. 2012. "Physical Punishment of Children: Lessons from 20 Years of Research." *Canadian Medical Association Journal* 184 (12): 1373–77. https://doi.org/10.1503/cmaj.101314.

"Early Brain Development and Health." 2022. Center for Disease Control And Prevention (CDC): https://Www.Cdc.Gov/Ncbddd/Childdevelopment/Early-Brain-Development.Html March 25, 2022.

Fivush, Robyn, Marshall Duke, and Jennifer G. Bohanek. 2010. "Do You Know..." The Power of Family History in Adolescent Identity and Well-Being," February.

Fox, Julia. 2016. "Poor Parenting Can Be Passed From Generation to Generation: Study." NBC News: Https://Www.Nbcnews.Com/News/Amp/Ncna566036. May 2, 2016.

Fredrickson, B L. 2001. "The Role of Positive Emotions in Positive Psychology. The Broaden-and-Build Theory of Positive Emotions." *The American Psychologist* 56 (3): 218–26. https://doi.org/10.1037//0003-066x.56.3.218.

Gershoff, Elizabeth T., and Andrew Grogan-Kaylor. 2016. "Spanking and Child Outcomes: Old Controversies and New Meta-Analyses." *Journal of Family Psychology* 30 (4): 453–69. https://doi.org/10.1037/fam0000191.

Gershoff, Elizabeth T., Andrew Grogan-Kaylor, Jennifer E. Lansford, Lei Chang, Arnaldo Zelli, Kirby Deater-Deckard, and Kenneth A. Dodge. 2010. "Parent Discipline Practices in an International Sample: Associations With Child Behaviors and Moderation by Perceived Normativeness." *Child Development* 81 (2): 487–502. https://doi.org/10.1111/j.1467-8624.2009.01409.x.

Ginsburg, Kenneth R. 2011. "Independence, One Step at a Time." Https://Www.Healthychildren.Org/English/Ages-Stages/Teen/Pages/Independence-One-Step-at-a-Time.Aspx. September 8, 2011.

Gonzales, Sasha. 2019. "How Children Pick up on Parents' Anxiety and Anger and Why We Should Be Mindful of How We Act." Https://Www.Scmp.Com/Lifestyle/Health-Wellness/Article/3012143/How-Children-Pick-Parents-Anxiety-and-Anger-and-Why-We. May 29, 2019.

Grady, Jessica Stoltzfus. 2019. "Parental Gentle Encouragement Promotes Shy Toddlers' Regulation in Social Contexts." *Journal of Experimental Child Psychology* 186 (October): 83–98. https://doi.org/10.1016/j.jecp.2019.05.008.

Kelly, Jane. 2020. "Study: Overbearing Parents Lead To Long-Term Struggles With Relationships, Education." Https://News.Virginia.Edu/Content/Study-Overbearing-Parents-Lead-Long-Term-Struggles-Relationships-Education. June 17, 2020.

Klahr, Ashlea M., and S. Alexandra Burt. 2014. "Elucidating the Etiology of Individual Differences in Parenting: A Meta-Analysis of Behavioral Genetic Research." *Psychological Bulletin* 140 (2): 544–86. https://doi.org/10.1037/a0034205.

Lara, America, Antonio Crego, and Martin Romero-Maroto. 2012. "Emotional

Contagion of Dental Fear to Children: The Fathers' Mediating Role in Parental Transfer of Fear." *International Journal of Paediatric Dentistry* 22 (5): 324–30. https://doi.org/10.1111/j.1365-263X.2011.01200.x.

Le, Bonnie M., and Emily A. Impett. 2016. "The Costs of Suppressing Negative Emotions and Amplifying Positive Emotions During Parental Caregiving." *Personality and Social Psychology Bulletin* 42 (3): 323–36. https://doi.org/10.1177/0146167216629122.

Lee, Lewina O., Peter James, Emily S. Zevon, Eric S. Kim, Claudia Trudel-Fitzgerald, Avron Spiro, Francine Grodstein, and Laura D. Kubzansky. 2019. "Optimism Is Associated with Exceptional Longevity in 2 Epidemiologic Cohorts of Men and Women." *Proceedings of the National Academy of Sciences* 116 (37): 18357–62. https://doi.org/10.1073/pnas.1900712116.

Lee, Shawna J., Catherine A. Taylor, Inna Altschul, and Janet C. Rice. 2013. "Parental Spanking and Subsequent Risk for Child Aggression in Father-Involved Families of Young Children." *Children and Youth Services Review* 35 (9): 1476–85. https://doi.org/10.1016/j.childyouth.2013.05.016.

Milkman, Katy. 2021. *How to Change: The Science of Getting from Where You Are to Where You Want to Be.* Portfolio.

Sege, Robert D., Benjamin S. Siegel, Emalee G. Flaherty, Amy R. Gavril, Sheila M. Idzerda, Antoinette "Toni" Laskey, Lori Anne Legano, et al. 2018. "Effective Discipline to Raise Healthy Children." *Pediatrics* 142 (6). https://doi.org/10.1542/peds.2018-3112.

Siegel, Daniel J., and Mary Hartzell. 2013. *Parenting from the Inside Out: How a Deeper Self-Understanding Can Help You Raise Children Who Thrive.*

Soto, Christopher J., and Joshua J. Jackson. 2013. "Five-Factor Model of Personality." In *Psychology.* Oxford University Press. https://doi.org/10.1093/obo/9780199828340-0120.

The Science of Kindness | Cedars-Sinai. "The Science of Kindness | Cedars-Sinai," February 2019. https://www.cedars-sinai.org/blog/science-of-kindness.html.

Tomoda, Akemi, Hanako Suzuki, Keren Rabi, Yi-Shin Sheu, Ann Polcari, and Martin H. Teicher. 2009. "Reduced Prefrontal Cortical Gray Matter Volume in Young Adults Exposed to Harsh Corporal Punishment." *NeuroImage* 47 (August): T66–71. https://doi.org/10.1016/j.neuroimage.2009.03.005.

Wang, Ming-Te, and Sarah Kenny. 2014. "Longitudinal Links Between Fathers' and Mothers' Harsh Verbal Discipline and Adolescents' Conduct Problems and Depressive Symptoms." *Child Development* 85 (3): 908–23. https://doi.org/10.1111/cdev.12143.

Weir, Kirsten. 2020. "Nurtured By Nature ." *American Psychological Association* 51 (3).

Sources

Winston, Robert, and Rebecca Chicot. 2016. "The Importance of Early Bonding on the Long-Term Mental Health and Resilience of Children." *London Journal of Primary Care* 8 (1): 12–14. https://doi.org/10.1080/17571472.2015.1133012.

Made in United States
Troutdale, OR
11/20/2023

14756923R00116